One Plus One Equals One

Bible Discussions
for Married Couples

Andrew T. Le Peau
Phyllis J. Le Peau

InterVarsity Press
Downers Grove
Illinois 60515

© 1981 by Inter-Varsity Christian Fellowship of the United States of America

All rights reserved. No part of this book may be reproduced in any form without written permission from InterVarsity Press, Downers Grove, Illinois.

InterVarsity Press is the book-publishing division of Inter-Varsity Christian Fellowship, a student movement active on campus at hundreds of universities, colleges and schools of nursing. For information about local and regional activities, write IVCF, 233 Langdon St., Madison, WI 53703.

Distributed in Canada through InterVarsity Press, 1875 Leslie St., Unit 10, Don Mills, Ontario M3B 2M5, Canada.

Study nine is adapted from Jesus: One of Us, IVP (1981).

The quotation on page 55 is from Harold Myra's poem "Divorce" in Love Notes to Jeanette, © 1979 by Harold Myra and used by permission.

ISBN 0-87784-803-3

Printed in the United States of America

19	18	17	16	15	14	13	12	11	10	9	8	7	6	5	4	3	2
95	94	93	92	91	90	89	88	87	86	85	84	83	82				

Part I.   Expectations in a Marriage   9
   1. Well, What Did You Expect?   *11*
   2. Loving Yourself—Psalm 139   *16*
   3. One Family under God—Psalm 128   *20*
4. One Plus One Equals One—Genesis 1:26-31; 2:15-25   *24*

Part II.   The Making of a Marriage   29
   5. Two to Submit— Ephesians 5:21-33   *31*
   6. Being the Servant—Philippians 2:1-11   *35*
   7. As Blood Is to the Body—Ephesians 4:1-3, 25-32   *39*
8. Drink Deeply, O Lovers—Song of Solomon 4:1—5:1   *44*
   9. The Extent of Forgiveness—Matthew 18:21-35   *49*

Part III.   Pressures on a Marriage   55
   10. Until Divorce Do Us Part—Matthew 19:1-12   *57*
   11. Self-Serve—Luke 22:14-27   *61*
   12. The Harried Married—Psalm 23   *65*
   13. Rebellious Children—Luke 15:1-2, 11-32   *69*
   14. Money, Possessions, Security—Matthew 6:19-34   *74*

Part IV.   The Foundations of a Marriage   79
   15. Priorities in Marriage—Genesis 2:18—3:24;
                  Mark 1:21-39   *81*
   16. Love Is—1 Corinthians 13   *85*
         Appendix: Planning in Marriage   *89*
                  Leader's Notes   *106*

Abbreviations

Foulkes
The Epistle of Paul to the Ephesians by Francis Foulkes (Grand Rapids, Mich.: Eerdmans, 1956).

Glickman
A Song for Lovers by S. Craig Glickman (Downers Grove, Ill.: InterVarsity Press, 1976).

Martin
The Epistle of Paul to the Philippians by R. P. Martin (Grand Rapids, Mich.: Eerdmans, 1959).

Morris
The Gospel according to Luke by Leon Morris (Grand Rapids, Mich.: Eerdmans, 1974).

NBC
The New Bible Commentary: Revised edited by D. Guthrie, J. A. Motyer, A. M. Stibbs and D. J. Wiseman (Grand Rapids, Mich.: Eerdmans, 1970).

NBD
The New Bible Dictionary edited by J. D. Douglas (Grand Rapids, Mich.: Eerdmans, 1962).

Tasker
The Gospel according to Matthew by R. V. G. Tasker (Grand Rapids, Mich.: Eerdmans, 1961).

Trobisch
I Married You by Walter Trobisch (New York: Harper and Row, 1971).

Introduction

A friend of ours once said, "One of the most helpful things you ever told me was that prayer was work. That set me free in prayer in a fresh, new way. I stopped feeling spiritually deficient and guilty because prayer wasn't coming naturally for me. I didn't have to work up or wait for the right mood to sweep me away into prayer. I just dug in my heels and had at it. What a relief to find out there wasn't something wrong with me. Prayer was work!"

We hope this guide will have the same effect for many in their marriages, for marriage is work. A minister pronouncing two people husband and wife does not create instant intimacy. Intimacy comes from hours of talking together about ideas and feelings, from months of learning more about each other's backgrounds and upbringings, from years of carefully observing how each other acts and reacts in a variety of circumstances. Marriage is work.

Many are discouraged because they are no longer swept away into close communion with their mate. They try to work up or wait for the right mood, but it comes all too infrequently. But there is nothing wrong with them. Marriage is work. Knowing this can free them to dig in their heels and have at it. For it takes work to listen when you think you have something more important to say. It takes work to help your spouse be financially responsible when you like new things too. It takes work to get up with the kids at night when you have had a hard day. Marriage is work because love is work.

Love is work because love, contrary to popular belief, is not simply emotion. It is action. "Love is patient and kind; love is not jealous or boastful; it is not arrogant or rude. Love does not insist on its own way; it is not irritable or resentful; it does not rejoice at wrong, but rejoices in the right. Love bears all things, believes all things, hopes all things, endures all things" (1 Cor 13:4-7). Love is work.

This guide is an opportunity for you to work at your marriage. It comes in the form of sixteen discussions for one couple or for a group of couples. The first four discussions in part one set the stage by covering expectations in marriage— our expectations of ourselves and of our families as well as God's expectations of us. The five studies in part two move into the areas of basic, hard labor in marriage—submission, servanthood, communication, sex and forgiveness. These are often the most difficult aspects of life together.

Part three begins five discussions of pressures on marriage with a look at divorce. While divorce may result from internal weakness stemming from a neglect of the basics considered in part two or from external pressures covered in the rest of part three, divorce is also a pressure in its own right. It is sweeping into every corner of society. Christians and non-Christians alike are affected. We also hope that discussing self-centeredness, busyness, rebellious children and insecurity can help prepare couples to deal with them before any becomes an active issue.

The last part returns to the foundations on which the house of marriage rests. First, priorities, those few crucial aspects of marriage which are not to be neglected if the house is to stand. (The appendix then gives some practical helps in making these priorities part of your daily routine.) Then last, love, the work which binds the entire marriage together.

Not all the passages we have selected deal primarily with marriage. But each one teaches principles that apply to marriage. Our intent is not to make the Bible say things it doesn't but to shine its light on important areas of married life.

This guide follows the Revised Standard Version of the Bible, though it is adaptable to other translations. If you are using the guide in a group, however, you will find it helpful for all to use the same version. In general a modern translation is recommended rather than a paraphrase or an older, archaic version. Your group may also find it helpful for each couple to work through each discussion before the group meets. Couples can then note in the guide the insights of others from the group discussion. The group leader will find practical suggestions for getting the most out of each group discussion in the back of the guide.

Marriage is work, but it brings joy and true intimacy, just as prayer brings us joy and binds us to the One who made marriage.

Part I

Expectations
In a
Marriage

---

*Expectations sit so quietly on
our shoulders, so lightly
around our belts and seclude
themselves so unobtrusively
in our pockets that we are
unaware of their presence. Unless, check list in hand, we
inspect ourselves to bring hidden
expectations to light, they
will victimize us mercilessly.*

John White, *Parents in Pain*

Study 1

Well, What Did You Expect?

Expectations are funny things. Depending on your expectations, the same event can make you gloriously happy or terribly depressed. If a presidential candidate expects to do very poorly in a primary and gets 45% of the vote, he will be elated even though his chief rival received over half the vote. On the other hand, if he expected to win by a landslide and garners only 55% to his opponent's 45%, his run for office may be near its end. In the first case, he actually lost, but it was perceived as a victory. In the second, the victory was seen as a loss. It all depends on expectations.

The same is true in marriage. If a couple agrees to "relax" next Saturday, one may anticipate a day together or an extended picnic while the other looks forward to a day for each to wrap around a novel. Result: either a great argument will arise come Saturday or at the least the picnic-expecting spouse will be disgruntled at not being able to get his or her mate out from behind the book. So what was to be a good day for both is soured by expectations.

And why this tug of war? Perhaps because of another funny thing about expectations. Often they are unspoken. And often a person isn't even aware of his or her own expectations. The purpose of the following exercise is therefore to help you verbalize your expectations on some basic issues regarding married life. We hope this will be an education for both you and your spouse.

A word of caution, however, before you begin. This discussion is not meant to provide a debating forum so you can try to convince each other that your expectations are morally superior, more practical or just better all around. Rather we want to provide an opportunity for you to understand each other better.

We suggest that husband and wife write their responses to the following questions independently (on separate sheets of paper if you have only one copy of this guide). After this you can spend time discussing your answers, asking each other to expand points you don't fully understand. While this may give you a base for compromise, remember the main point is not to come to a mutual agreement on what your expectations should be, but simply to discover each other's expectations. So be prepared to do lots of listening.

---

1. What do you think are the most important things for each of the following to do and to be?

A woman—

A wife—

A mother—

A man—

A husband—

A father—

---

2. What values do you think are most important to pass on to your children and why? (You may want to think in the following categories: people, religion, work, play, friends, family, money, race, war and peace, possessions, education, politics and so on.)

---

3. What expectations do you have of children—whether you have any or not? (You may want to think in one or more of the following categories: relating to you as parents, relating to friends of theirs and of yours, chores, church, school, money, relating to their siblings and so on.)

---

4. What would you like most for your children to become (whether you have any or not)?

5. What makes an ideal family for you?

For Family Discussion
As a couple, ask your children (if you have any) the following questions and note down their answers. While it may be better to interview the children one at a time so they don't influence each other's answers, it might not hurt to do it together as a family since children (especially young children) will be quite honest no matter who is around or what has already been said. You and your spouse will then want to discuss their answers privately. (Note: Even if one or more of your children is quite young, as long as they can make sentences, you should ask them these questions.)

6. What do you want most from your dad?

7. What do you wish your dad wouldn't do?

8. What do you want most from your mom?

9. What do you wish your mom wouldn't do?

10. What do you want most from each of your brothers and sisters?

11. What do you wish each of your brothers and sisters wouldn't do?

12. What is a good family like?

Study 2

Loving Yourself

Psalm 139

Any good thing can be twisted or distorted or inflated or reduced in such a way that it is no longer good. If you are over-
weight, food is not necessarily good for you. If you are on
top of a skyscraper, diving into a pool may not be good for
you. But food and diving are good—in their proper contexts.
Love of self is also susceptible to perversion. There can be
too much self-love as well as too little. Psalm 139 can help us
put self-love in its proper setting.

Notes on the Text

139:5 *layest thy hand upon me*—the Good News Bible trans-
lates this, "you protect me with your power." The
NBC (p. 538) comments on this verse, "Such knowledge as God possesses of us could be a terrifying
thing, but it is here allied to a protective purpose."

139:8 *Sheol*—the word used in the Old Testament for the
abode of the dead.

139:14 *fearful and wonderful*—KJV and RV translate this, "I
am fearfully and wonderfully made."

1. Why is it important in a marriage to love yourself?

What can happen if you don't?

---

2. Read Psalm 139. What are the indications in this passage of God's love and concern for us?

---

3. In verses 1-6 what does it mean to be known by God?

Do you want to be known by God? Why or why not?

What fears are there in being known?

---

4. What evidence is there that you need not be afraid to be known by God?

---

5. God is concerned to know all about us. How can we also get to know ourselves and help our mates to know themselves?

---

6. In verses 7-12, what evidence is there that God is ever present?

What difference does it make to you that God is ever present?

7. In verses 13-18, for which of God's creative works is the psalmist praising God?

What is the content of the psalmist's prayer of praise?

8. What are we saying about God's creation if we don't like who we are?

9. Look at verses 19-22. How might this situation have caused the psalmist to wonder how important he was to God?

10. In verses 23-24, what can be the value of knowing your own "wicked ways"?

11. In summary, what difference does it make to you that you are important to God?

In what ways can you grow in healthier self-love?

12. How can you help your mate have healthier self-love?

For Further Study
Walter Trobisch, *Love Yourself* (Downers Grove, Ill.: Inter-Varsity Press, 1976).
Richard Peace, *Learning to Love Ourselves* (Downers Grove, Ill.: InterVarsity Press, 1968).

Study 3

One Family under God

Psalm 128

The pursuit of happiness may be an unalienable right, but pursued for its own sake happiness generally eludes us. The wisdom writers of the Bible saw clearly that happiness (or blessedness, as they more often called it) comes to us as a by-product of making other things our goal. Psalm 128 helps us to see what makes for a happy household.

Notes on the Text

128:1   *fears the* LORD—reverence for and trust in God.

128:3   *a fruitful vine . . . olive shoots*—wine and olive oil, the products of the vine and olive tree, are signs of God's blessing (see Deut 8:8 and Hos 2:22).

128:5   *Zion*—probably the name of the hill on which stood the Jebusite fortress in Jerusalem or the name of the fortress itself (captured by David and referred to as the city of David in 2 Sam 5:7); the term was also used to refer to Jerusalem itself.

1. What do you think makes a happy husband?

2. Read Psalm 128. What does the psalmist say makes a happy husband?

3. What does it mean to fear the Lord?

Would you say *fearing the Lord* is the same thing as *walking in his ways?* Why or why not?

4. How much of your happiness comes from obeying God?

5. In verses 2-4, what sources of happiness does the psalmist say spring out of obedience to God?

6. What makes work satisfying?

Comment on the following statement: If a person is in a right relationship with God, his work is likely to be more satisfying.

7. To what does the psalmist compare a wife?

List several characteristics of a fruitful wife.

Husband, how would a wife with these characteristics appeal to you?

Wife, how would you evaluate yourself on these characteristics?

Husband, how might (or does) a right relationship between you and God affect your wife?

8. What do you think the psalmist is trying to communicate by calling children "olive shoots"?

What is the significance of the children being around the table?

9. Verses 5-6 close the psalm in a benediction. How does this prayer place the family in a larger context?

How is your family affected by the circumstances of the nation you live in?

10. Verse 6 declares, "May you see your children's children!"—not necessarily a common occurrence among ancient peoples. Why might your life be extended by living obediently toward God?

11. The psalmist says that living in harmony with God will produce a happy life. What steps can you take to make your household happier?

For Further Study
Eugene Peterson, *A Long Obedience in the Same Direction* (Downers Grove, Ill.: InterVarsity Press, 1980), pp. 109-18.
Jim Conway, *Men in Mid-Life Crisis* (Elgin, Ill.: David C. Cook, 1978).

Study 4

One Plus One Equals One

Genesis 1:26-31; 2:15-25

Independence. Countries fight for it. Financially we strive for it. Saying you are in need is not an easy thing to do. All of which makes the popularity of marriage a little mysterious, unless there really is a place for interdependence in human relationships.

Notes on the Text

1:27 *male and female*—to establish God's original purpose in marriage, Jesus refers to this passage when answering the Pharisees' question about divorce (Mt 19:4). Study ten will take up the Matthew 19 passage as a whole.

2:18, *helper*—a subordinate role is not necessarily implied by
20 this word. Note that in Exodus 18:4; Psalms 33:20; 70:5; 115:9, 10, 11; 121:2; 124:8 and 146:5 God is called the help of Israel.

2:23 *she shall be called Woman*—this is a word play in Hebrew, just as in English, as the Hebrew for man ('*îš*) sounds like the Hebrew for woman ('*iššâ*).

2:24 *Therefore a man . . .* —this passage is quoted by Jesus in Matthew 19:5 (see study ten). It is also found in Mark 10:7 and Ephesians 5:31 (see study five).
one flesh—"Of course, 'to become one flesh' means more than just physical union. It means that two persons share everything they have . . . that two persons be-

come completely one with body, soul and spirit and yet there remain two different persons" (Trobisch, p. 18).

1. In what ways do husbands and wives depend on each other?

2. Read Genesis 1:26-31. In what ways, according to this passage, are human beings like God?

3. How does the combination of maleness and femaleness together reflect the image of God?

4. Why is it significant that male and female are to work as a team to accomplish the tasks God has given them?

What implications does this have for you and your spouse in relating to singles?

5. In what ways do you and your mate work as a team in your marriage?

6. Read Genesis 2:15-25 noting that this takes place prior to the Fall. Looking at verses 15-17, what is Adam's relationship with God like?

7. In verses 15-20, what is Adam's relationship with nature like?

8. In all of Genesis 1—2, what is unique in verse 18 about God saying, "It is not good"? Why is this significant?

9. Looking at verses 21-25, how was Eve a companion for Adam in ways that God or nature was not?

10. What three actions are stressed in verse 24?

11. In what senses should you leave your parents when you marry?

What are some consequences of cleaving to your mate?

What are the implications of being one flesh?

12. What happens if any one of these three parts is missing in your marriage?

In which of these three areas are you strongest? Why?

In which are you weakest? Why?

How might you work to strengthen this area?

For Further Study

Walter Trobisch, *I Married You* (New York: Harper and Row, 1971), especially pp. 11-24.

Part II

The Making of a Marriage

Dialogue is to love, what blood is to the body. When the flow of blood stops, the body dies. When dialogue stops, love dies and resentment and hate are born. But dialogue can restore a dead relationship. Indeed, this is the miracle of dialogue: it can bring relationship into being, and it can bring into being once again a relationship that has died.

Reuel L. Howe, *The Miracle of Dialogue*

Study 5

Two
to Submit

Ephesians 5:21-33

A lot of emotion and misunderstanding surround the word *submit*. Undoubtedly some of both has tainted us otherwise thoroughly rational creatures—would you believe partially rational? In any case, try to set aside your own bias and see what Paul has to say about submission. Come to the text as if you had not seen it before. Then you may be able to accurately view your own perspective with fresh eyes.

Notes on the Text

5:24　　 *subject in everything*—"does not mean . . . that she is in the hands of one who has authority to command what he pleases. She is to be submissive to one whose duty to her is expressed in nothing short of the highest demand of self-giving love. Her subjection in the light of this, and in the light of the high ideal of unity that is to be expressed in verses 28-31, is such that" it cannot be considered humiliating (Foulkes, p. 157).

5:25, 28 *love*—the Greek *agapaō* is used, meaning totally unselfish, self-giving love.

5:31　　 *For this reason . . .*—Genesis 2:24 is quoted by Paul to root his arguments about the unity of husband and wife in creation itself (see study four and study ten).

1. Read Ephesians 5:21-33. How does verse 21 preview the whole passage?

2. How does Paul say wives are to submit to their husbands?

What does it mean to submit to the Lord?

3. List the ways Christ has authority over the church.

Why does Christ have authority over the church?

What does this have to do with the husband-wife relationship?

4. Wives, how could your submission to your husband grow more like your submission to Christ?

5. List the ways Christ shows love for the church.

List the ways husbands show love for their wives.

6. Husbands, how could your love for your wife grow more like that of Christ for the church?

7. How do verses 31-33 summarize the teaching on mutual submission?

8. Why do you think Paul calls on wives to *respect* their husbands while he calls on husbands to *love* their wives?

9. Wives, how can you show more respect to your husbands?

Husbands, how can you show more love to your wives?

Note that verses 22-24 are instructions *to wives* in how they are to conduct themselves in marriage. They are not instructions to husbands on how they are to make their wives behave or on what they have a right to expect. Likewise verses 25-30 are instructions *to husbands* in how they are to conduct themselves in marriage. They are not instructions to wives on how they are to make their husbands behave or on what they have a right to expect. Paul emphasizes the responsibilities of each and makes no comment on the rights of either. In light of this we hope that in questions 4, 7 and 9 that husbands did not respond if wives were addressed or vice versa. The intent was for both to consider for themselves what their responsibilities are and how to respond.

For both husbands and wives the responsibility is to submit to each other, though Paul sees this acted out in different ways. Submission in either case, however, is counting others better than yourself. Paul calls on both husbands and wives to do this—husbands especially submitting to their wives by loving them and meeting their needs; wives especially submitting to their husbands by respecting them and honoring them as their head. The next study gives you an opportunity to explore in greater detail what submission means for both of you by considering the ultimate example of submission that we are to emulate—Jesus Christ.

For Further Study
John Stott, *God's New Society: The Message of Ephesians* (Downers Grove, Ill.: InterVarsity Press, 1980), pp. 213-36.

Study 6

Being the Servant

Philippians 2:1-11

Whether male or female, in an age of self-assertiveness, few of us are interested in being servants. But this is what the Bible calls us to. Perhaps because the notion is so unpopular and distasteful, it is worth the effort to look more closely at the kind of servant Jesus was, the kind of servant we are to imitate in all our relations with others, including marriage.

Notes on the Text

2:3 *count others better*—Paul is not saying that others are better than oneself (obviously everyone couldn't be better than everyone else) but that we should conduct ourselves, should act, as if other people were of higher value. By doing this, we will end up treating others just as we should. The same balance is found in verse 4.

2:6 *did not count equality with God a thing to be grasped*—"The eternal Son of God . . . renounced what was his by right . . . and chose instead the way of obedient suffering as the pathway to His Lordship" (Martin, p. 99).

1. To review the last study, what does it mean that Christ gave up his life for the church?

2. Read Philippians 2:1-11. According to verses 1-2, what should be the foundations of our life in Christ?

What is the outcome of this life in Christ that Paul desired?

What role do these foundations play in marriage as well?

3. What practical suggestions does Paul go on to give that make this life possible (vv. 3-4)?

With which of these do you have the most difficulty? Why?

How did Christ count others better than himself?

4. Paul again uses Christ as the ultimate example of humilty and servanthood, as he did in Ephesians 5. How is Christ's basic attitude toward himself described in verses 5-6?

How did he act out this attitude (vv. 7-8)?

What were the results of his actions (vv. 9-11)?

5. How does this description of Jesus expand on the thought of "giving up his life for the church"?

6. As you consider what kind of servant you are in your marriage, what is your basic attitude toward yourself?

How do you live out this attitude in relationship to your spouse?

What are the results of your actions?

7. What difference might it make in your marriage if you attempted to take on Christ's mind?

8. Take five minutes to write answers privately to the following: What practical ways can I be a servant to my spouse this week?

Now take five minutes to talk over this list with your spouse.

Study 7

As Blood Is to the Body

Ephesians 4:1-3, 25-32

When God wanted to speak as clearly as possible to the ones he loved, he sent his Son who was full of grace and truth. When we want to speak as clearly as possible to the one we love, we also want to be full of both. But as with many goals and desires, this is often difficult to implement. The aim of this study is to bring us at least a few steps closer.

Note on the Text

4:26 *Be angry but do not sin*—"The Christian must be sure that his anger is that of righteous indignation, and not just an expression of personal provocation or wounded pride. It must have no sinful motives nor be allowed to lead to sin in any way" (Foulkes, p. 133).

1. Reuel L. Howe says in *The Miracle of Dialogue*, "Dialogue is to love, what blood is to the body." What does it mean to dialogue?

What, then, does Howe's statement mean to you?

What are some of the strengths and weaknesses of your communication with your spouse?

2. Read Ephesians 4:1-3, 25-32. Paul is so concerned for these Christians that he *begs* them to lead a life worthy of their calling to Christ. How should they do this according to verses 1-3? Give a short phrase to describe each aspect.

3. Think of a couple you know who exemplifies these characteristics. What is their marriage like?

4. Looking on to verses 25-32, why is it important to speak the truth with your spouse (v. 25)?

What hidden or covered-up resentments, subjects, ideas or problems in your relationship do you need to discuss?

Why is it important in marriage to "not let the sun go down on your anger" (v. 26)?

5. What types of communication would you classify in your marriage as "evil talk" (v. 29)?

Does this mean that painful subjects should not be raised? Explain.

Verse 29 might be summarized:
    1) Say only what will build up the other person.
    2) Say only what suits the occasion.
    3) Say only what will bless the other person.
How would these guidelines be helpful for a discussion of some difficult topic?

6. How does one "grieve the Holy Spirit" (v. 30)?

How does broken communication in your marriage affect your communication (relationship) with God?

7. How does one put away bitterness, wrath, anger, clamor, slander and malice (v. 31)?

In what specific ways can you be more kind and tender-hearted toward your spouse (v. 32)?

8. How has God in Christ forgiven you (v. 32)?

How can you contribute toward a greater spirit of forgiveness within your family?

9. In this study we discussed several aspects of communication and of handling conflict. Write a few practical steps you could take this week to improve communication with your spouse.

Now discuss your lists together.

For Further Study
David Augsburger, *Caring Enough to Confront* (Glendale Calif.: Regal, 1973).
Judson Swihart, *How Do You Say, "I Love You"?* (Downers Grove, Ill.: InterVarsity Press, 1977).
Paul Tournier, *To Understand Each Other* (Atlanta: John Knox, 1967).

Study 8

Drink Deeply, O Lovers

Song Of Solomon 4:1—5:1

The Bible is a realistic book. It does not shy away from any important issue in life. King Solomon's love song to his bride offers a beautiful and frank expression of physical love in marriage. Yet his song does not isolate and exalt sex as a goddess the way our culture does. Rather it delights in the love that God has given to a husband and wife.

Notes on the Text

4:1   *a flock of goats*—"One imagines these black goats covering the hillside in the same way the Shulammite's black locks fall gently down from the crown of her head and over her back" (NBC, p. 583).

4:4   *the tower of David*—"The Shulammite's neck is like a tower adorned with trophies. The whole verse indicates regality of bearing" (NBC, p. 583).

4:8   *Come with me from Lebanon*—"The dens of lions and the mountains of leopards were fearful places to the north, perhaps near her homeland. In asking her to come from such fearful places, he is really asking her to bring her thoughts completely to him and leave her fears behind and perhaps to leave the lingering thoughts of home behind as well" (Glickman, p. 19).

4:12   *a garden locked*—"The exclusiveness of the relationship [is] denoted by this delightful phrase" (NBC, p. 584).

4:13 *Your shoots*—"the expressions of her lovely personality. This phrase is the subject of all that follows in vv. 13-15" (NBC, p. 584).

1. What is your attitude toward the physical aspects of sex in your marriage?

2. Read the Song of Solomon 4:1—5:1. Who is speaking in 4:1-15?

3. In 4:1-7, what aspects of his bride does the husband describe?

What is he trying to communicate by the different images?

How do you feel when your mate tells you how physically desirable you are?

4. What invitation does the husband make in 4:8?

5. What reasons beyond physical beauty does he then give for wanting her (4:9-15)?

How important is it to you to hear your spouse say, "I love you"? Explain.

6. How would you characterize the wife's answer to her husband's invitation (4:16)?

Why has she withheld nothing from him?

7. Why is it important to prepare for sex the way the husband and wife do here in this passage?

What problems can arise if a husband and wife do not prepare in this way?

8. How do you feel about having sex when you are not emotionally ready?

What prepares you emotionally for sex?

---

9. Do you believe sex is one of your rights in marriage? Why or why not?

Does the husband in this passage *act* like it is one of his rights? Explain.

---

10. What attitude toward sex is expressed by the last part of 5:1, "Eat, O friends, and drink: drink deeply, O lovers"?

What is the significance of such a positive view of sex being in the Bible?

---

11. How, if at all, does the attitude the Bible expresses here toward sex affect the attitude you expressed at the beginning of the study?

How might this change your sex life with your spouse?

For Further Study
James Dobson, *What Wives Wish Their Husbands Knew about Women* (Wheaton, Ill.: Tyndale, 1977).
S. Craig Glickman, *A Song for Lovers* (Downers Grove, Ill.: InterVarsity Press, 1976).
R. C. Sproul, *Discovering the Intimate Marriage* (Minneapolis: Bethany, 1975).
Ingrid Trobisch, *The Joy of Being a Woman* (New York: Harper and Row, 1975).
Ingrid Trobisch and Jean Banyolak, *Better Is Your Love Than Wine* (Downers Grove, Ill.: InterVarsity Press, 1971).

Study 9

The Extent
of Forgiveness

Matthew 18:21-35

Forgiveness is crucial to any ongoing relationship. But what do you do, especially in a marriage, when the offense is particularly great? Jesus' parable of the unforgiving servant can shed some light on how we should respond.

Notes on the Text

18:22 *seven times*—symbolic, not literal, in meaning; Peter is asking, in effect, whether there should be any limit to his forgiveness.

18:23 *kingdom of heaven*—the reign of God over the new community of people which Jesus brought into being by saving them through his death.
servants—"high-placed officials in the service of the emperor, some of whom would often have occasion to borrow large sums from the imperial treasurer" (Tasker, p. 178).

18:24 *talent*—about fifteen years' wages; the full amount stresses the inability of the servant to pay.

18:25 *to be sold*—a common way to deal with a debtor's default on debts was to sell him and his family into slavery.

18:27 *out of pity*—this phrase is perhaps more clearly translated by KJV and NASB as "was moved with compassion" and "felt compassion."

18:28 *denarii*—one denarius was worth a day's wage; the

amount owed is small enough that with patience one could hope to recover it.

1. How would you describe a marriage in which there is little or no forgiveness?

2. Now read Matthew 18:21-35. Behind Peter's question in verse 21 was the Jewish teaching that you need forgive someone only up to three times. So then what do you think was Peter's attitude here?

3. If you had been Peter, how would you have reacted to Jesus' reply in verse 22?

What keeps husbands and wives from forgiving each other more freely?

4. Not content to let the matter rest with forgiveness seventy times seven, Jesus proceeded to elaborate his statement with a parable. Why did the king in the parable originally forgive the servant's debt?

Why do you forgive the wrongs of your spouse?

5. What was your first reaction to the behavior of the servant who forced his fellow servant to pay back his debt? Why?

6. Do you think the king's punishment of the servant was justified? Why?

Why ought the servant to have forgiven his fellow servant's debt?

7. Compare the character of the king with that of the unforgiving servant.

8. In this parable who does the king represent?

Who do the servants represent?

What does the servant's great debt to his lord represent?

9. What does it mean to forgive another "from the heart"?

What does Jesus say our situation is if we do not forgive another?

10. How does this story answer Peter's question?

11. What kind of debt do we owe to Christ?

How can we repay it?

12. How can forgiving one another frequently be important in maintaining a healthy marriage?

What have you not yet forgiven your spouse for?

Talk these over now with your husband or wife.

For Further Study
David Augsburger, *The Freedom of Forgiveness* (Chicago: Moody, 1973).
Francis A. Schaeffer, *The Mark of the Christian* (Downers Grove, Ill.: InterVarsity Press, 1970).

Part III

Pressures on a Marriage

*"You know, it could happen
to us," you said to me. . . .
"You're right," I finally admit.
We've never joked about
divorce, never brought it up as an
option. We declared total
commitment to each other and
must reaffirm that always.
But maybe realizing it could
happen to us helps us make sure
it won't.*

Harold Myra, *Love Notes
to Jeanette*

Study 10

Until Divorce Do Us Part

Matthew 19:1-12

Momentum is a word sportcasters delight in using to describe the team that's on the move, that's controlling the game. They may be behind now, but they will probably win. In the struggle between marriage and divorce in our society today, divorce seems to have the momentum. And while many couples may have been swept into matrimony on a wave of romance, only a few years or even months later, divorce has the momentum with them too. It is important for the couple who want to keep a strong marriage to discuss divorce when it seems theoretical and distant. For when love appears to be weakening and tensions are on the rise, it may be too late. In fact, that is why we have placed this discussion of divorce before those of other pressures on a marriage.

Notes on the Text

19:4-5 *Have you not read . . . ?*—Jesus goes on to quote Genesis 1:27 and 2:24, taking "them back behind the law . . . to the creation which showed that the two sexes were according to the purpose of God" (NBC, p. 840).

19:7-8 *Moses command . . . Moses allowed*—Both Jesus and the Pharisees refer to Deuteronomy 24:1-4 in which a man was *permitted* to divorce his wife, not *required* to as the Pharisees say.

19:9 *unchastity*—"The word *porneia . . .* is a comprehensive word, including adultery, fornication and unnatural vice" (Tasker, p. 184).

19:12 *eunuch*—can mean either a court officer or one who has been castrated, though here it obviously refers to those who are celibate either by their choice or without it.

1. Would you ever get a divorce? If so, for what reasons? If not, why not?

What binds husbands and wives together in marriage? (Money? Love? Children? Something else?)

2. Read Matthew 19:1-12. Contrast why the crowd came to Christ with why the Pharisees came.

With which group do you identify more as you approach Christ?

3. In your own words, state Christ's answer to the question the Pharisees raise about divorce.

What does "two shall become one flesh" mean (v. 5)?

4. How has God joined a husband and wife together?

In what ways are husbands and wives divided?

5. How does Christ respond to the Pharisees' next question?

What does he mean by "hardness of heart"?

How do you tend to be hard of heart in your marriage?

6. Why do the disciples respond as they do in verse 10?

7. The disciples' alternative to not divorcing was not to marry. Why does Jesus say this view is inadequate (vv. 11-12)?

So what alternative does that leave for married couples?

8. The disadvantages of saying that divorce would never be an option were rather obvious to the disciples. Discuss the advantages to you and your spouse of determining never to divorce.

For Further Study
Jim Conway, "Divorce ... & You," HIS magazine, April 1979, pp. 1-8.
Jim Conway, "A Meeting of Needs," HIS magazine, February 1980, pp. 16-20.

Study 11

Self-Serve

Luke 22:14-27

Maybe hanging together in marriage is tougher than it might look at first because our society doesn't offer much help on how to hang together. More is said and written about self-help and self-improvement than about how to help others, even those in your own family. This study is designed to give you a chance to see how much this trend affects your marriage.

Notes on the Text
22:25 *those in authority over them are called*—the pagan kings " 'get themselves called'... benefactors.... Men of the world like to receive credit for what they have done" (Morris, p. 308).
22:26 *the youngest*—since age carried with it a position of honor in ancient societies, the youngest would then have the least honor.

1. What makes it so difficult to sacrifice for the good of others?

2. Read Luke 22:14-27. Describe the situation in verses 14-23.

What do you think Jesus is feeling at the Last Supper?

3. How sensitive are the disciples to what Jesus is saying and feeling (v. 24)?

Why do you think they reacted this way?

4. How do you react in your family when a crisis hits?

Why do you respond as you do?

5. What do you think it meant to the disciples to be great?

What does our culture say greatness is?

What do you think it means to be great?

6. How does Jesus define greatness?

7. Would you say our society is more oriented to self-improvement or to serving others? Why?

How could your family orient itself more toward serving others?

8. How can you better serve each other in your marriage? Be practical.

What obstacles will you have to overcome?

9. How would Jesus have lived in this age of me-ism?

How can we as followers of Christ influence this kind of society?

For Further Study
Howard Guinness, *Sacrifice* (Downers Grove, Ill.: Inter-Varsity Press, 1976).

Study 12

The Harried
Married

Psalm 23

How busy we all are! Housework, office work, yard work, church work, work on the car, social engagements, out-of-town company. And then there's the kids' schedules on top of that! What a contrast David's life seems to be as he describes it in Psalm 23!

Notes on the Text

23:2 *still waters*—generally sheep will not drink from running water but only from quiet pools. Finding water and green pastures is also no easy task in a dry and stony land.

23:5 *oil*—a sign of God's blessing, health and happiness. In ancient societies, if your face glistened (as with oil) it meant you ate well. And if you ate well, you were one of the wealthy ones.

---

1. How would you define "the harried life"?

How harried a life do you live?

Why do we live such harried lives?

---

2. Read Psalm 23. How does verse 1 summarize the whole psalm?

How do you respond to such a statement? Does it seem real to you or is it just words?

---

3. According to verses 2-3, what needs does the shepherd meet? What do each of these mean?

---

4. Of those mentioned, which do you think is your greatest need? Why?

---

5. What else, according to verse 4, does the shepherd offer?

What is meant by the "shadow of death"?

How have you experienced his presence through the "shadow of death"?

6. What does a shepherd do with a rod and staff?

How would this be a source of comfort and protection for the sheep?

Where do you most need the Lord's discipline?

7. According to verse 5, what else does the Lord do for us? What do each of these mean?

How are you enjoying his table?

8. How does verse 6 summarize the psalm?

How does this psalm contrast with our harried lives?

9. What needs to happen in your life before the shepherd can meet your needs as described in this psalm?

For Further Reading
Charles Hummel, *Tyranny of the Urgent* (Downers Grove, Ill.: InterVarsity Press, 1967).

Study 13

Rebellious Children

Luke 15:1-2, 11-32

God is a parent who has dealt with rebellious children for thousands of years. The parable of the lost son tells us how he responds as a parent to children who reject him and his ways. We can learn from his example.

Notes on the Text

15:1 *tax collectors and sinners*—while taxation was controlled by the foreign power of Rome, natives of a given province often acted as collectors. The hate they incurred from their countrymen was due to both their dishonesty and their disloyalty to the homeland. This hate was aggravated for strict Jews, like the Pharisees, because they were ceremonially unclean from their continual contact with Gentiles (NBD, pp. 1064-65).

15:12 *the share of property that falls to me*—in Jesus' day, one could leave his wealth either through a will (in which case one retained both capital and income till death) or through a gift (in which one would give the capital but still receive any income it earned till death). So while the younger son's request was not unheard of, his attempt to use the capital indicated he was treating his father as though he were dead (see Morris, p. 240).

15:16 *pods*—seeds from carob trees (see Morris, p. 241).

15:31 *all that is mine is yours*—note that the father divided his property between his sons (v. 12). So to each he gave part of his capital, retaining control over the income (see note above).

1. How do you usually respond when your children rebel against you?

2. Read Luke 15:1-2, 11-32. How would you characterize the father's response to the younger son's request?

3. Why do you think the father responds as he does?

Do you think he knows how his son will handle the inheritance?

4. How would you have responded if you were the father? Why?

5. What are the advantages of allowing children the freedom to make mistakes?

How much of this kind of freedom do you offer your children?

6. After he has squandered his inheritance and is destitute, what does the younger son finally decide to do?

What indications are there that he is truly repentant?

7. How does the father respond to his son's return? (Consider specific acts as well as attitudes.)

8. How willing are you to forgive your children?

How do you express your forgiveness?

9. In verses 25-32, how is the rebellion of the older son different from that of the younger?

How is it similar?

10. Who initiates reconciliation in each father-son conflict?

How can you initiate reconciliation more frequently with your rebellious children?

11. The parable, of course, is a look at how God relates to his people. What kind of picture of God is portrayed here?

12. With which son do you most identify in your relationship with God? Why?

How does this parable say God has acted toward you?

What then is your response to him?

For Further Study

David Augsburger, *Caring Enough to Confront* (Glendale, Calif.: Regal, 1973).

David Augsburger, *The Freedom of Forgiveness* (Chicago: Moody, 1973).

Ross Campbell, *How to Really Love Your Child* (Wheaton, Ill.: Victor, 1977).

John White, *Parents in Pain* (Downers Grove, Ill.: InterVarsity Press, 1979).

Study 14

Money, Possessions, Security

Matthew 6:19-34

We often hear that this is the age of materialism—if not capitalist then communist. This study is to help us evaluate how much the world has pressed us into its mold on this count.

Notes on the Text

6:22-23 *sound ... not sound*—one English word (*sound*) is used in translating two different Greek words. First, *haplous* (v. 22) and other forms of the word are translated elsewhere in the New Testament as "generosity" (2 Cor 9:11, 13), "generously" (Jas. 1:5) and "liberality" (Rom 12:8; 2 Cor 8:2). In three other cases it is used in the context of giving full allegiance or devotion, that is, single-mindedness (Eph 6:5; 2 Cor 1:12; 11:3). The remaining case is the passage in Luke (11:32) that is parallel to Matthew. The second word, *ponēros*, is translated many times as "evil," and also as "malice," "wickedness" and even "envy." In Mark 7:22 (KJV) and Luke 11:34 it is used in reference to an evil eye, "a Jewish metaphor for 'a grudging or jealous spirit' " (Tasker, p. 76). In Matthew 20:15 and Luke 11:13 it is also used in contrast to generosity. Therefore, Christ is likely using the metaphor of the eye to contrast generosity and grudgingness.

6:24   *mammon*—a transliteration from the Aramaic, mean-
        ing wealth; but Christ uses it to say that "when a
        man 'owns' anything, in reality it owns him" (NBD,
        p. 775).

1. Could you live on half your present income? Why or
why not?

2. Read Matthew 6:19-34. How does Jesus contrast earthly
riches and heavenly riches?

3. What does Jesus mean by "riches in heaven"?

What pressures do you feel from TV advertising and other
sources to store up earthly riches?

4. What is your family doing to store up each kind of treasure?

5. Look at verse 21. What difference would it make if Jesus had said instead, "Where your heart is, there will your treasure be also"?

6. In light of how the notes on page 74 explain the terms *sound* and *not sound*, how do verses 22-23 fit in this passage about money and possessions?

7. Why does Jesus say you can't serve two masters (v. 24)?

Do you think you can serve both God and money? Why or why not?

8. What reasons does Jesus give for not worrying about food and clothes (vv. 25-34)?

How can these comments on the birds and the flowers help you overcome your worry about these things?

9. How would you contrast a household that is mostly concerned about earthly treasure with one that is mostly concerned with heavenly treasure?

10. In verse 34, why does Christ say we should not worry about tomorrow?

What do you worry about most in regard to the future?

What difference is there between worrying about the future and planning for the future?

How can this passage help you become more secure?

For Further Study

George Fooshee, *You Can Be Financially Free* (Old Tappan, N.J.: Revell, 1975).

Ronald J. Sider, *Rich Christians in an Age of Hunger* (Downers Grove, Ill.: InterVarsity Press, 1977).

Simon Webley, *How to Give Away Your Money* (Downers Grove, Ill.: InterVarsity Press, 1979).

Part IV

The Foundations of a Marriage

Over the years the greatest continuing struggle in the Christian life is the effort to make adequate time for daily waiting on God, weekly inventory, and monthly planning. Since this time for receiving marching orders is so important, Satan will do everything he can to squeeze it out. Yet we know from experience that only by this means can we escape the tyranny of the urgent.

Charles Hummel, *Tyranny of the Urgent*

Study 15

Priorities in Marriage

Genesis 2:18—3:24; Mark 1:21-39

Pressures on a marriage can mold it into something neither husband nor wife want. But holding vigilant watch against these pressures is not always enough. We also need to state positively what we want our marriage to be and then strive constructively toward those ends.

Notes on the Text
Genesis
2:24 *Therefore a man...*—"In this key verse about marriage, quoted four times in the Bible, there is not one word about children.... Leaving, cleaving, and becoming one flesh are sufficient. Full stop. Even if there are no children the one-flesh union does not become meaningless" (Trobisch, pp. 20-21).
Mark
1:21 *Capernaum*—a city on the northwest shore of the Sea of Galilee.

---

1. How do you determine what your priorities should be in your marriage?

2. Read Genesis 2:18—3:24. Describe the relationship God and Adam had before Genesis 3.

3. Focusing on 2:24, what priority should parents take in relation to one's mate?

By inference, what priority are children to be in relation to one's mate?

4. What strategy did the serpent use to deceive Eve?

5. Adam decided to disobey God. To what did he give priority over God?

6. In verse 8, what changes have taken place in Adam and Eve's relationship with God from what it was in Genesis 2?

7. What were the consequences of Adam and Eve's giving something other than God priority in their lives?

8. To what do you give greater priority than you do to God? (Spouse? Children? House? Career? Cars? Wealth?)

What might be the consequences of this?

According to this passage, your spouse is to have priority over your parents and children while God should come before even your spouse. When one of these relationships is disturbed, all of the other relationships go out of kilter as well.

9. Read Mark 1:21-39. What activities was Jesus involved in in Capernaum?

What demands were placed on him?

10. Why would it make sense for him to stay in Capernaum rather than leave?

What did he say was his priority (v. 38)?

11. How does it appear that Jesus decided what he should do?

What evidence is there that it was Jesus' routine to rise early and pray?

12. What role does prayer have as you set your priorities?

What steps can you take to give prayer itself a higher place in your life?

13. This week, take an hour as a couple to pray over your priorities and then write down your basic conclusions. (The appendix offers many more hints on how to set priorities and act on them.)

For Further Study
Charles E. Hummel, *Tyranny of the Urgent* (Downers Grove, Ill.: InterVarsity Press, 1967).

Study 16

Love Is

1 Corinthians 13

This is the last study in our series on marriage. We've discussed expectations, pressures, forgiveness, being a servant and priorities. In 1 Corinthians 13 we will consider love which is both a roof over and a foundation under these other aspects of marriage.

Notes on the Text
13:1 *love*—not a humanistic or romantic ideal but God's love which we are able to share and express to others selflessly.

13:7 *believes all things*—love is always ready to see the best in a person and to give that person the benefit of the doubt.

13:10 *when the perfect comes*—when the end of human history is reached, all that is partial will pass away and be replaced with full understanding.

1. How would you define love?

2. Read 1 Corinthians 13. What spiritual gifts does Paul mention in verses 1-3?

How does he contrast these with love?

3. Why are these gifts valueless without love?

What talents or gifts would be useless in marriage without love? Why?

4. In verses 4-8, what does Paul say love is and is not?

5. What is meant by "love does not insist on its own way"? Give some examples of this in marriage.

6. What is meant by "love does not rejoice at wrong" (v. 6)? What are some examples of this in marriage?

7. Which aspect of love listed do you most desire to show?

Which aspect do you have the most difficulty giving?

8. Paul talks about the eternal quality of love in verses 8-12. With what does he contrast it?

9. Why do you believe he says that love is the greatest of faith, hope and love (v. 13)?

10. How would Paul respond to this definition: Love is a warm feeling in your heart?

Can one practice love without a "warm feeling"? Why or why not?

11. What are some practical steps you can take to show more love toward your spouse?

According to Paul, love is *doing* what is right and good for the benefit of others. It is not necessarily something one *feels*. It may mean doing what you know to be right in spite of how you feel. Our effectiveness as Christians is determined by how we show love and not by our leadership skills, knowledge, wealth or anything else. The same is true in marriage.

For Further Study
Lewis B. Smedes, *Love within Limits: A Realist's View of 1 Corinthians 13* (Grand Rapids: Eerdmans, 1978).

Appendix

Planning in Marriage

For months we had waited for John and Patti to visit. John was Phyllis's cousin (like a brother) and Patti was her matron of honor (like a sister). Andy got to know them later, of course, but they soon became close. Their company was stimulating, their openness was refreshing, their humor was delightful. They were close friends who had moved to California while we were in Chicago. So there had been little opportunity to be with them recently. Their three-day stay with us, then, would be very special.

It was a disaster. Four months later we were still picking up the pieces, trying to glue back together the vase of our friendship that somehow had been dropped and whose flowers now lay wilting on the floor. What had happened?

John and Patti's visit was on our calendar for months. It was a priority for our fall, an event to anticipate, to look forward to. But in the six weeks prior to their visit, several other items got onto our calendar as well: Andy had two out-of-town trips, and the two of us together had another. We had three sets of overnight company, leaving only four evenings at home alone as a family. And Phyllis was pregnant, due to deliver Susan in a month. By the time John and Patti arrived, our "priority" weekend with them had been reduced to fourth class. We had no energy left to give them, and they saw that. They felt that they had become unimportant to us because we were so obviously unprepared for them. We had blown it.

The unfortunate incidents, the misunderstood exchanges, the hapless miscues and miscellaneous things gone wrong piled so high that by the time John and Patti left, it was possible we would never see them again over that manmade mountain of mistakes. Our close friends were in great danger of becoming truly distant relatives. Why? Because we had not saved our time, our energy, ourselves for what was truly important to us. We had allowed a hundred sundry demands, desires and duties to walk unhindered into our lives and crowd out our friends. Through several long phone calls, letters and the asking for and receiving of forgiveness, the relationship was restored. But we vowed to ourselves that we would be far more vigilant to prevent the unimportant from again dominating our lives. It almost cost us a friendship. Next time it could cost more.

We have, in fact, tried to do this since we were first married, though (as you have seen) with varying degrees of success. Each fall we try to take at least two uninterrupted days without children to plan for the coming year. We pray. We study the Bible together. Then we try to write out our priorities, not only for finances and vacations, but also for our social calendar, our church commitments, and our personal spiritual, physical and emotional well-being.

When we tell people that we do this, we get a variety of reactions.

"You must be kidding!"

"I don't do anything in life planned."

"I never thought about planning my marriage. I wouldn't even know how to begin."

"I don't plan very often because if I say, 'This is going to happen,' and it doesn't, I can't cope with not having my expectation met."

In our marriage, planning has been a positive experience. Our goals give us guidelines as to what our priorities will be for each coming year. Of course we have frustrating days in which everything is twisted inside out with nothing happening but changing diapers, answering the phone and flopping into bed, and we ask, "Have I accomplished anything?" It is helpful emotionally at such times to realize we are aiming toward something for the year, that in the long run we are at least hitting some of our priorities, that not all is in vain. Having long-term goals assures us that we are doing some things that truly matter.

Our plans are not perfect. Inevitably, if we are on our way out the door to give a talk on planning, one of us can't find the right shoes, Susan and Stephen have decided this is the time to resist the cultural bias toward being dressed and the bath tub gets stopped up. We are still learning and growing.

Some people ask if planning is unspiritual. Doesn't it crush the possibility of being led by the Holy Spirit day by day if you've already decided how each day will go? Remember what James said, "Come now, you who say, 'Today or tomorrow we will go into such and such a town and spend a year there and trade and get gain'; whereas you do not know about tomorrow." But of course James goes on to say, "Instead you ought to say, 'If the Lord wills, we shall live and we shall do this or that.' " That is the point: Will we plan apart from God or under his loving eye?

We don't need to plan in order to crush out the Spirit, either. We can do that quite well without a plan. Likewise we can be guided by the Spirit whether or not we have set goals. Our conclusion is that both kinds of guidance are legitimate, that they complement one another. In Proverbs 16:3 it says, "Commit your ways to the Lord and your plans will be established." If we come to God, placing all of our activities in worship at his feet, he will give us a sense of priorities and the means to live by those priorities. He will establish our plans. He will see to it, by his Holy Spirit, that the plans he gives us will mesh with his own eternal plan.

God has had a plan from eternity past that he intends to

carry through eternity future. What is his plan? "For he has made known to us in all wisdom and insight the mystery of his will, according to his purpose which he set forth in Christ as a plan for the fulness of time, to unite all things in him, things in heaven and things on earth" (Eph 1:9-10). He intends to unite all things in Christ. And he has been working this out slowly, step by step, calling Abraham, preparing a people to receive the law, giving them the prophets, preserving the royal line through which Messiah would come, creating a culture and government that would allow the gospel to spread with astounding speed, building his church to await his coming again.

He has a timetable, you see. He has not chosen to do everything at once, instantaneously, though he could have. Rather each part of the plan has its proper place in its proper time. All these and more he planned and accomplished with more yet to come—the ultimate goal being to bring the whole created universe under Christ's lordship. In the context of God's cosmic plan, by the guidance of the Holy Spirit, we then seek to bring all that is in our lives under Christ's lordship so that he can establish our plans in accordance with his. We do not plan in isolation from God, but we plan on the stage of the eternal drama the Lord is producing. God has chosen to work out his plan through people. He could have done it all himself, but he includes us. So, in one way, our life here on earth is a time to get our plans lined up with his.

Many in the Bible made their plans in this way, small parts of the larger whole. Joseph devised a fourteen-year plan (Gen 41) of storing and then rationing grain so that Egypt would not be decimated by a seven-year famine. God used this to preserve the people of Israel out of which the promised Messiah was to come.

Moses followed the advice of his father-in-law (Ex 18: 13-27) and divided the work of judging the people, delegating authority to commanders of tens, fifties, hundreds and thousands. This freed Moses to concentrate his efforts on the most important tasks God had given him rather than being buried by an avalanche of minor problems.

Nehemiah, after prayer and fasting, offered a step-by-step plan to a foreign king on how the walls of Jerusalem might be built with the king's help. The king accepted the proposal and God worked through this to re-establish the city in which Christ would die to reconcile the world to himself.

Our Lord himself, on the night before he died, thanked his Father that he had accomplished all that his Father had given him to do (Jn 17:4). Think of it! What would it be like to say at the end of your life, "Father, I've been so in tune with you throughout my life that I've finished exactly those things which you determined ahead of time that I was to do—not those things I set for myself to do, and not what everyone else said that I should accomplish, but what you determined for me"? Did Christ heal all the lame in Palestine? Did he preach to all the people of Israel? No. Yet he had finished what was important, the priorities, the things that mattered, that which his Father gave him to do.

All of us can have that same sense of direction in life, that same assurance of doing the primary things God wants us to do without the fear that we, like Moses, will be overwhelmed by the trivial.

Planning, knowing God's priorities and making them ours, is thus one outworking of a close walk with God. Yet even this is itself an act of obedience to God. For the Lord commands us to "seek first his kingdom and his righteousness, and all these things shall be yours as well" (Mt 6:33). Find God's priorities and do them. Then all the other needs of life will follow.

"But in the next verse Jesus tells us not to worry about tomorrow. Isn't planning just a sophisticated way of being anxious about the future?" No. Worrying about tomorrow and thinking about tomorrow are two very different activities. We are told elsewhere, in fact, that we are to think about, to pray about, to look forward to the day when God's plan will be completed at the return of Christ (Rev 22:20). No, Jesus is suggesting we look forward in faith to what tomorrow will hold—a day when he will provide all our needs as we set our hearts firmly on his will—rather than fretting and drumming our fingers because we lack the faith to believe he will provide if we obey.

Planning, committed to God, can then be an act of faith in what God will do. It is seeing the future consequences of today's choices. It is calmly, quietly, consciously making decisions under God that are too important to make under the crush of circumstances. Christ did not give in to circumstances as he faced the cross. He stuck to God's eternal plan and drank the cup the Father gave.

Planning is deliberately giving the Holy Spirit an opportunity to direct our path. Not planning could mean that when the car needs a new clutch and the roof starts to leak and Harry breaks his arm, the church won't get its tithe. Not planning could mean that when the neighborhood co-op needs a new treasurer and the Sunday school needs a new superintendent and the grade-school basketball team needs a new coach, your family won't get the time it needs. The pressures of the immediate crush out what the Holy Spirit wants to tell you is important. Long-term decisions are not made in the midst of a series of short-term crises.

Is the neighborhood co-op a good thing? Is the basketball program? Is the Sunday school? Certainly. Life is full of good things—many good things. So many, in fact, that there are more good things to do in life than there are resources of time, energy, ability or wealth with which to accomplish them. Which of the good things will you do? God wants you to commit yourself to what is best.

Should the roof get fixed? If not, the whole house will rot. Should Harry's arm have a cast? If it doesn't, the complications could be worse. But if you've decided ahead of time that you will give a tithe, then a leaky roof or a broken arm will not interfere. Maybe, though, you will have to postpone a new color TV and stick with the black-and-white.

Much of our decision making, then, will be deciding what we will not do. For example, in our marriage, we have decided to sing in the church choir but not to participate in any choir extracurriculars (banquets, bake sales and the like). We feel that participating in worship this way is important for us but that the other activities are not. We have other outlets for service and socializing.

We have also decided we will lead a Sunday-school class but that we will not serve on any church committees or boards. Nonetheless, each time we have been asked to do so, we have not dismissed the offer out of hand. Rather we have thoughtfully prayed and reconsidered whether or not this was the time to change our decision. Each occasion thus far we have reaffirmed our choice not to join committees—as attractive as they sound for serving the church in new ways. We believe God wants us to focus our efforts in the church on the Sunday-school class.

For several years we have wanted to begin a neighborhood Bible study. We seemed to be in an ideal situation for one—a block of close, friendly people. Reluctantly, however, we concluded that our other obligations made this unrealistic. So for several years we decided not to attempt such a study, though we continued to pray about it regularly. In the meantime, God was preparing the way. He was building several relationships in a new way, in a way that they did not exist four years ago. And suddenly with great ease, we have a thriving neighborhood study.

Choices are inevitable, whether they are made ahead of time or on the spot. Not so long ago people were quite fond of quoting Camus who said, "Not to decide is to decide." The statement is still true. If you do not decide, circumstances or other people will decide for you. And they may not be deciding according to God's will. Circumstances led David into two opportunities to kill King Saul. But he had already decided to follow God's command and not to murder the Lord's anointed. Herod allowed Herodias and social pressure to decide the fate of John the Baptist, not having decided ahead of time what he should do (Mk 6:11-29).

Some may wonder by now if we really believe something we said several pages back: the Spirit can guide in both long-term and on-the-spot decisions. It is our understanding and experience that he usually wants to guide in both. Why shouldn't he? God wants to teach us to trust him moment by moment and for all of eternity.

There will come times when plans must be set aside. Richard, the head of a national Christian ministry, was once preparing to direct a key conference. Then he received a phone call. A friend in town had died suddenly. The man's daughter asked Richard to preach at his funeral. Richard laid aside his work and went directly to the family. Though the conference was only a couple days off and he had planned to spend those days in final preparation, he not only preached, he spent those days with those who needed the time more than he did.

The Spirit may also show us at some later date that our plans need to be changed. We don't need to be locked for a month or a year into a plan that should be changed. Rather we should do just that—change the plan, again as God directs. Neither are we suggesting that every minute of every day needs to be planned. People need to be spontaneous for psychological as well as for spiritual reasons. We are suggesting, rather, that everyone at least ought to plan enough so that what is truly important to God is not left behind.

We have said that planning is deciding ahead of time to do what is most important in God's eyes, saying no even to what is good in order to say yes to what is best. How do we go about planning? As we said earlier, we begin with prayer and Scripture, looking to God together as a couple. There is much good material written to guide study and prayer, so we need not discuss them in detail. Suffice it to say, if you are able to spend two days planning, the first hour of each could profitably be spent together in the Bible with prayer punctuating your activity throughout the day.

There are many good methods for planning and decision making. We have found the four-step approach summarized in Table 1 to be helpful.

Table 1
Developing a Plan in Marriage

Step One. What is the overall goal or purpose for our marriage?

Step Two. What is life like for us now?

1. What am I like?
2. What is our family like?
3. What is our community like?
4. What is our nation like?
5. What is our world like?

Step Three. What would our ideal family be like?

1. What will fulfill us?
2. How will we stand in contrast to the world around us?
3. How will we meet the needs around us?
4. How will we fit into God's ideal for us?

Step Four. How will we move our family from what it is like now toward the ideal?

1. Brainstorm a list of alternatives, withholding judgment as we ask, What are our possible activities, goals, resources?
2. Categorize alternatives into three to six groups such as financial, social, sexual, emotional, intellectual, etc.
3. Evaluate the alternatives, asking: Is it realistic? Does it contribute to our overall goal and ideal? Should we postpone it? Do we have or can we get the necessary resources?
4. Assign responsibilities and work out the details.
5. Put it all on a calendar.

This process is slow and time-consuming. But it assures us that we have talked about our life together as completely as possible.

If you decide to use the plan in Table 1, we recommend that before you begin you have what we call a "garbage session." In planning you will be sharing intimately and intensely. You will be disagreeing at times as well. If there are unresolved issues, feelings or problems between you before you begin, your planning could be counterproductive.

To help air feelings of which you may not even be fully aware, we suggest you ask yourselves the questions in Table 2.

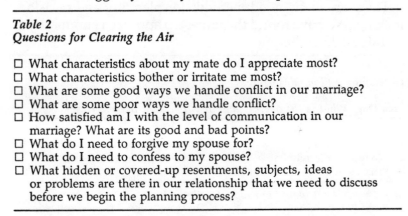

Table 2
Questions for Clearing the Air

☐ What characteristics about my mate do I appreciate most?
☐ What characteristics bother or irritate me most?
☐ What are some good ways we handle conflict in our marriage?
☐ What are some poor ways we handle conflict?
☐ How satisfied am I with the level of communication in our marriage? What are its good and bad points?
☐ What do I need to forgive my spouse for?
☐ What do I need to confess to my spouse?
☐ What hidden or covered-up resentments, subjects, ideas or problems are there in our relationship that we need to discuss before we begin the planning process?

You may be able to think of other questions that would fit you more appropriately than those in the table. By all means, ask them, as long as the air is clear between you before you move on. It is our experience that couples that do not do this are often stymied in their planning until they finally have a garbage session—be it formal or informal! Better to do it first than last.

Step one of the planning process itself (Table 1) will probably take the least amount of time of the four steps: *What is the overall goal or purpose for our marriage?* Write out in a sentence what you see to be the main direction you want to head in. It could be cast in terms of Genesis 2:24, such as, "To leave our parents, cleave to each other and become one flesh." Or it might read, "By God's grace, to help each other and those near us to become more like Christ in the situation God has put us in." Or, as the Westminster Shorter Catechism puts it, "To glorify God and enjoy him forever." In any case, it should be simple and straightforward, and it should express the way you perceive your life together. Don't spend too much time fussing over details. Your overall goal should be general and broad. But do take enough time to discuss what you see as important and come to a common statement of that. You can always come back to this later and make some adjustments as you see the need.

Step two will take more time, perhaps one, two hours or more: *What is life like for us now?* You want to try to gather as much information or make as many intelligent guesses about your life as you can, even if it seems trivial. It is on the basis of this information and these assumptions that you will make decisions later on.

One easy way to do this is to answer the questions in Table 1.

1. What am I like? (Consider background, education, family, likes, dislikes, strengths, weaknesses, etc.)

2. What is our family like? (See below.)

3. What is our community like? (Consider population, ethnic make-up, financial condition, location, character, educational system, cultural and recreational opportunities, history, etc.)

4. & 5. What is our nation/world like? (A broad question that may seem impossible to answer, but even if you don't have the facts, it is necessary to make certain assumptions about what your country and the world will be like in the coming year if you are going to plan in it. Obviously if your assumptions prove wrong, your plans will change. You don't know for certain that the economy will be essentially stable in the next year, but for the moment, you do need to start somewhere. Consider also politics, religion and other areas.)

You will want to spend more time answering question two on your marriage and family than on the other questions. So you may want to ask and answer some of the following:

What is the spiritual life of our family like? (Consider personal prayer life, Bible study, times of family prayer, church involvement, service to others, tithing, etc.)

How is the physical well-being of those in our family? (Consider diet, amount and frequency of exercise, weight, frequency and length of vacations, days off, etc.)

How are our family finances? (Consider debts, income, budget—if we don't have a budget, why don't we?—contributions, etc.)

What is our social life like? (Consider friends, organizations or clubs belonged to, etc.)

What are our jobs like? (Consider type of work—office work, physical labor—degree of satisfaction, what makes it good or not so good, division of labor around home, etc.)

How is our family's emotional health? (Consider how much we practice confession and forgiveness, how well we communicate with each other—husband with wife as well as parents with children—what kind of relations we have with relatives and in-laws, what crises our family has gone through recently, etc.)

What intellectual, cultural and recreational experiences is our family having? (Consider how much we read, watch TV, go to sporting events, plays, movies, the symphony, etc.)

All this fact gathering may seem boring and unimportant. But before you can get to Brooklyn, you have to know whether you're in Bombay, Berlin or Buenos Aires, what kinds of transportation are available and how much money you have. To say "I'm going to Brooklyn" without doing a little research first may only find you frustrated, tired and in Berlin.

Not all the information you gather will prove valuable. But you won't know which is important and which isn't unless you get the full picture provided by going through the whole process. If you don't price the market for used cars, you won't know a good deal even if it runs you over. So bear through this research stage even if it drags. The investment will definitely be repaid.

In step three you backtrack a bit and dream a lot. Having discovered what your family is like, ask yourselves, *What would our ideal family be like?* While in step two you sought out limits, here you assume there are no limits on your resources of time, money, talent or on the Holy Spirit's ability to work in you. If your family could be anything (athletic, wealthy, forgiving, peaceful, helping, quiet), what would it be? If you could develop any skills (reading, car repairing, harp playing, surfing, counseling, farming), what would they be? If you could be any kind of person (content, fun-loving, intellectual, humorous, courageous, steadfast, happy-go-lucky), what would you be? What would truly gratify you, satisfy you, fulfill you? How will you stand in brilliant contrast to the dark world you looked at in step two? How will you pour your healing arts into the world's most serious wounds? Who does God want you and your family to be? What is his ideal?

"But alas and alack," you say. "The real and the ideal are eons apart." This then is the purpose of step four and the heart of planning: *How will we move our family from what it is like now toward the ideal?* Begin by brainstorming. This is like step three in that you assume no limitations, but it can be more specific. Just start listing on a piece of paper the various ways you could work (partially or completely) toward fulfilling the ideals you set in step three. If one ideal was to be a helping family, list all the different kinds of ways you could learn to grow in that area. Don't evaluate your ideas yet. Don't consider how far-fetched, unrealistic or impossible they may seem—or even if they fit your ideal all that well. Write all your ideas down as fast as they come to you. The reason for this is to help you be creative by not fearing judgment on what you say. Some—no, most of your ideas will be impossible. But a few will be creative solutions that might not have come out if you kept assuming the normal limitations of life.

Ask yourself these three main questions: What are possible activities? What are possible goals? What are possible resources?

Next categorize these ideas into three to six major groups. Most people tend to think in terms of financial, spiritual, vocational, social, sexual, emotional and intellectual areas. Pick the ones that seem to fit you best.

Now you can evaluate. The following questions can help: Can we realistically (in terms of time, money and talent) do this in the next year? Will it contribute toward our overall goal (step one) or to our statement of the ideal (step three)? Is this something that is worthwhile but that we will just have to put off for another year?

Cross off those items you decide against. Transfer to another list those that you must postpone for a year or more. (You can use that list next year when you work through the process again!) Then take what is left and start to work out the details. Suppose you want to read more Scripture as a family in order to promote your spiritual growth. Then you will need to decide how often you will do it, when you will do it, who will do it and what will be read. Another item you might keep on your list is "Less TV." What will the limits be? To whom do they apply? How will you enforce the limits? What will you substitute during the time otherwise spent in front of the tube?

After writing down the answers to these kinds of questions, you may begin to feel you've taken on too much. Fine. Eliminate a few more items from your list. You don't want to so overplan that you become overwhelmed and give up on everything. Better to plan a few things that you know you can accomplish and build from these.

Next, put everything on a calendar. Again, you may find or feel that there is too much. Don't hesitate to cut. Using a calendar is a concrete way of making sure we use the resource of time realistically.

Before you finish, you may also want to make a list of things you will *not* do—even if asked, or even if you want to do them. This has proved invaluable in our marriage, as we said above. It helps keep the top priority items at the top.

When you're all done, what you have left may look like something found in Table 3 or 4 (more likely 3 than 4!). Either form is acceptable—or a third form that suits the personality

Table 3
An Example of an Informal POGAS*

A. *Personal Spiritual Growth*
1. DAILY
   Pray as a couple five times/week
   At least one parent pray with each child at bedtime
2. WEEKLY
   Family prayer time once each week
   Sunday school each week
   Sunday worship each week
3. MONTHLY
   Tithe
4. QUARTERLY
   Review and revise this POGAS

B. *Physical Well-Being*
1. EXERCISE
   Volleyball each week as a couple
   Wife—daily exercises
   Husband—tennis once each week
2. DIET
   More vegetables, fewer starches
   6-8 glasses of fluids each day
   Second helpings only once/week
3. WEIGHT
   Maintain + or − 5 lbs. of current weight
4. VACATION
   One week at the lake in June
   One week at each set of grandparents before Thanksgiving

C. *Emotional/Family/Intellectual Health*
   Limit TV to 2 hours/day for children and 1 hour/day for us
   Go out as a couple (without children) at least once every
   two months
   Take one weekend without children in the next 12 months
   Read aloud to each other two books (one chosen by each) in
   the next six months
   Spend at least 2 hours of focused time with the children on
   weekends

**POGAS is derived from purpose, objectives, goals, and standards. "A* purpose *is a broad statement of an aspiration. It describes the general direction in which we desire to go. . . .*
   "An objective *is a more specific statement of an aspiration which, if attained, will produce progress toward fulfilling the purpose. . . . Or, looking at it in terms of problem solving, an objective is the solution to a problem.*
   "A goal *is a still more specific statement of what is to be accomplished to produce progress toward an objective. . . . Or, to continue the problem-solving perspective, a goal is the adequate testing of a possible solution to a problem.*
   "A performance standard *is a measurement by which performance can be evaluated. Standards can be expressed in terms which are relative to a purpose or an objective or a goal." From John W. Alexander,* Managing Our Work *(Downers Grove, Ill.: InterVarsity Press, 1975), pp. 18-19.*

Table 4
An Example of a Formal POGAS

Purpose: "A man leaves his father and his mother and cleaves to his wife, and they become one flesh" (Genesis 2:24).

Objective I:	To make sure our relations with our parents are on solid footing.
Goal A:	To learn what our relations with our parents are and should be.
Standard 1:	To ask each of our parents how they view our relationship with them in writing by May 1.
Standard 2:	To read *Passages* together by October 1, focusing on the stages our parents are moving through.
Goal B:	To seek to improve relations with our parents.
Standard 1:	To visit each set of parents at least once in the next 12 months.
Standard 2:	To write monthly to our parents, assuring them of our love each time.
Objective II:	To be submissive to one another (cleave).
Goal A:	To learn what it means to be submissive to each other.
Standard 1:	To read and discuss one Gospel, asking in each chapter, "How is Christ being a servant here? How can I follow his example?" One chapter per week beginning April 1.
Standard 2:	To ask my mate at least weekly, "What can I do to help you today?"
Goal B:	To act the role of a servant to my mate.
Standard 1:	Husband: Do dishes at least three times a week. Wife: Take out garbage every other week.
Standard 2:	To pray daily for my mate's specific needs.
Objective III:	To develop a mutually fulfilling sexual life (one flesh).
Goal A:	To learn what a mutually fulfilling sexual life is for us.
Standard 1:	To read one book aloud to each other on the sexual relationship in marriage by July 1.
Standard 2:	To ask each other at least every two months, "How sexually fulfilled are you these days?"
Goal B:	To remove hindrances to a mutually fulfilling sexual life.
Standard 1:	To be away from the kids two weekends in the next 12 months.
Standard 2:	To ask forgiveness for anything I have done to wrong my mate before engaging in sexual activity.

of your marriage better than either of these. The key is: it should be written and agreed upon by both of you.

Having signed your names to this formidable document, are you bound to it eternally? No, you are not even bound to it for the next year. Every few months, we try to take an evening to evaluate how we are doing on our plan, what goals need to be changed or deleted or added, and which ones we need to recommit ourselves to. The plan is intended to be a flexible tool, not a rigid taskmaster.

As we said, the method of planning just described is only one method we and others have found helpful. We encourage you to try it. But more important is that you find some way in your lives together to do those things God truly wants you to do and not to allow the pressures of guilt, circumstances or the expectations of others to force the important out of your lives.

Leader's Notes

Leading a group of married couples in a discussion of marriage can be exciting, rewarding, fulfilling and *terrifying*. You'll be asking people to share about one of the most personal aspects of their lives—a threatening prospect.

As you form your group you will want both to warn people what they are getting into and to let them know that they will not be pushed beyond what they want to express. But also let them know that open sharing can be the most helpful and encouraging aspect of a group using this guide.

How do you help create a group that has an open, accepting atmosphere? First, by being open about your marriage. (We encourage a couple to lead together.) Honesty is contagious. If you are willing to express your struggles and successes, others will be too.

Second, by being accepting of others. Acknowledge all contributions as legitimate positions. Do not reject any idea out of hand. Remember especially that you can't argue with feelings—so don't. In fact, allowing people to express feelings on topics they wouldn't ordinarily discuss (but should) can be beneficial. So help set the tone for the whole group by welcoming all comments. If the notion expressed is at odds with the Bible, either allow the rest of the group to respond with alternative ideas or take a few minutes at the end of the study to summarize a biblical position without singling out any one person or idea for attack.

Third, remember that this is not *your* group. It is the group's group—and God's. You are merely a facilitator of discussion rather than a teacher of facts. With a commitment to the Word of God and to helping others, your task is to guide the group to discover the truths in the Bible for themselves. That means you need to know your material well. You need to know where to lead them. Yet you will see that when people begin to discover Bible truths for themselves, excitement sets in which is followed by motivation. Your job then gets easier and easier as they begin to dig into the Word more and more with less direction from you.

How can you become a facilitator? *Pray*. Ask for the Spirit's illumination. God wants us to understand all of his Word, so you can confidently pray in his will. He also wants your group members to know him and his Word. Pray that God will help you be a facilitator, one who helps others grow in their own relationship with God.

Study. First move through each study yourself, noting the introductory material and the notes on the text. You might want to read through and take notes on the passage before you look at the questions in the guide, trying to understand it on your own first. A good rule of thumb is at least two hours of preparation for each study.

Prepare to lead. Only after you have completed your own study should you read through the leader's notes for the study you are working on. These are intended to warn you of potential problems in group discussion and to give you hints on how to bring out the essence of the passage. It is here too that you should take a close look at the purposes listed at the beginning of each section of the leader's notes. These are not necessarily meant to be read to your group. Rather these summarize what your group should take away with them. Now consider how each of the questions contributes toward accomplishing these goals.

You will note that each study contains some observation

questions (What does the passage say?), some interpretation questions (What does the passage mean?) and some application questions (What am I, or are we, going to do about this?). Don't be frustrated with the observation questions *even* if they seem unnecessary. If we are to interpret correctly, we must have a firm grasp of the content. This simply takes time and effort. Likewise, correct application requires correct interpretation. The interpretation questions could be the most interesting because they are discussion questions. Application questions might not elicit as much discussion because people can be threatened if responding requires them to admit problems or faults to the group. We all fear self-exposure! Be sensitive to such feelings while helping the group make specific application to their lives. The point of Bible study, after all, is that our lives be changed because we know God better.

There is a fourth type of question that is also used in this guide. Almost every study begins with one, two or three approach questions which are meant to be asked *before* the passage is read. These are very important questions, and we urge you not to skip them. Their intent is to help the group warm up to the topic. No matter how well a group may know each other or how comfortable they may be with each other, there is always a stiffness that needs to be overcome before people will begin to talk openly. Observation questions aren't very good for overcoming this. Second, approach questions get people thinking along the lines of the topic under discussion. Again, most people will have lots of different things going on in their minds (breakfast, an important meeting coming up, how to get the car fixed) that will have nothing to do with marriage. Again, as important as observation questions are, they can't solve this problem easily. Third, the answers given to the approach questions are built on later in most studies. This is why it is especially important *not* to read the passage before the approach question is asked. The passage will tend to color the honest reactions people would otherwise give because they are of course *supposed* to think the way the Bible does. Giving honest responses to various issues before they find out what the Bible says may well help them start to face the fact that they don't always think the way the Bible does.

Keep in mind, as you prepare to lead, that when you use published Bible study guides, the author is usually making a few unstated assumptions. We want to make at least one explicit: the author does not intend a group Bible-study leader to use the questions in the guide verbatim—in the order given, adding none, subtracting none. Rather, the questions and comments in the guide are intended to *guide* you through the passage. Like a map, they suggest a route to follow. But as with any map, neither is the traveler required to follow a certain path nor will all travelers take the same trip—even though they have the same map and may have the same destination. Some people like superhighways. Others are fond of side roads. Some may hit detours not noted on the map. Others may stop to sightsee along the way. But all use the map to meet their individual needs and desires.

The same is true with a Bible study guide (including this one). We assume you want to arrive at the ultimate destination outlined in the purposes given for each study in the leader's notes—and more generally that you want to help others develop stronger marriages in Christ. But you have one great advantage over us as you lead these studies. You know the people in your group and we don't. You will therefore have to adapt this guide (this map) to suit your needs.

First, your group may have certain needs not dealt with by this guide. You may have to add your own studies to fill in the gaps. We have tried to be complete and well balanced in our selection. But we know our choices will not suit everyone. In the course of the studies you may find, for example, greater needs in the area of child rearing than the one study in this guide can meet. That may mean you will need to look to other sources for help.

Second, your group may not be ready to broach certain topics in this guide. The studies on divorce or sex, for example, may not be appropriate for you. We have included them for those who are ready. Pray about whether or not yours is such a group.

Third, within each study you may find certain issues are not covered adequately for your group. Again, adapt. Write additional questions that will meet the need. Likewise, some individual questions may be too threatening. These too should be modified or deleted as is best for you.

Fourth, as each individual discussion progresses, you may find you can drop certain questions because adequate answers have already been given in response to previous questions. Do not feel compelled to proceed in lockstep fashion, asking all questions no matter what has been said previously. We, the authors, do not know exactly what will be said as you lead your discussion. (Neither do you!) But we have a general idea. (As you do.) Be sensitive to the flow of discussion as it takes place.

Likewise, a question in the guide may not elicit a full answer. You may then need to add two or three follow-up questions to bring it all out. Sometimes you can anticipate these ahead of time and write out some extra questions for options use.

Finally, we strongly encourage you to write out all questions and comments on a separate sheet of paper, putting it all into your own words. This will help make it your study, help you to be more at ease, and help discussion flow more naturally because you, the leader, are talking the way you normally talk and not the way Andy and Phyllis Le Peau happen to write questions.

As you lead the study discussion itself, you will want to keep the following in mind:

☐ Avoid answering your own questions. If necessary, rephrase them or ask, "Is the question clear?" Sometimes just repeating it will suffice. (The problem with answering your own questions is that discussion can be stifled if group members think the leader will do all the work for them or if they are threatened because the leader "knows so much and I don't want to show how much I don't know.")

☐ Similarly, don't be afraid of silence. Give the group time to look for answers. Remember it took you time to find the answers too.

☐ Don't be content with just one answer. Try to get several people to contribute to the discussion. Ask, "What do the rest of you think?" Even observation questions often have more than one answer.

☐ Acknowledge all contributions. Never refuse any answer. If a wrong answer comes up, ask, "Which verse led you to that conclusion?" or again, "What do the rest of you think?"

☐ Likewise, don't be afraid of controversy. It can be very stimulating. If you don't resolve an issue completely, don't be frustrated. Move on and keep it in mind for later. A subsequent study might solve the problem.

☐ Stick to the passage under consideration. Don't allow the group to hop through the Bible. If someone insists on cross-referencing where it is not essential, suggest a poststudy discussion of the matter. Or try asking, "Which verse in today's passage led you to that conclusion?"

☐ In the same way, stick to the topic under consideration. The questions will stimulate many ideas. Use the purposes at the beginning of each section in the leader's notes to guide you as to what is most relevant. But again be sensitive to the needs of individuals. Don't shut them off just for the sake of keeping a rule. Still, you might be able to deal with a person more openly after the study is over.

☐ Feel free to summarize, highlight background material (such as that found in the notes on the text) or review past studies. But don't preach.

☐ Pray before, after, or before and after each study. Probably afterward would be the best time for group conversational prayer.

☐ Begin and end on time.

Many more suggestions and helps are found in James F. Nyquist's *Leading Bible Discussions* (IVP). Reading and studying through that would be well worth your time.

Study 1. Well, What Did You Expect?

Purpose

☐ To aid couples in discovering what hidden expectations lie beneath their marriage and their family (if they have children).

Getting our expectations out cuts two ways: first, we deal with a source of tension by bringing expectations in the open where they can be looked at, talked about, explained, evaluated and changed; second, we create an opportunity for encouragement by discovering the needs of our spouse and then by doing something to meet those needs. If we have children, expectations cut the same two ways with them. Getting these in the open will also make us more prepared for the following discussions.

The key is to accept what people say. Remember, your goal as leader is to create an accepting atmosphere. Notice we don't say you must agree with what is said, only accept. Semantics? Not at all. To accept means to acknowledge the importance of others and therefore the importance of what they say. To dismiss what is said ("Oh, you don't really believe that?!" "Don't be silly!" "You think *what*?") is really to dismiss the value of the other person. To accept is to listen, to ask questions that will help people explain why they believe what they do ("What do you mean?" "Did your parents think the same way?" "Why do you believe that's so?"), and then to listen some more. Having accepted what a person has said, you are in a position to agree or disagree. And odds are you'll be listened to when you do.

Note that you will use only questions 1-5 in the group since questions 6-12 require a discussion with children.

Question 1. All this nice theory becomes instant practicality when you ask the first question. You may be in a homogeneous group that believes "a woman's place is in the home" and that "a man's place is on the job." But it's likely that you won't. Be prepared for a variety of answers. Refuse none. Remember, the purpose of this discussion is to help people express and thus discover their expectations so they can be dealt with. The purpose of the discussion is not to fill each other with buckshot. Some people may see no differences in the roles of men and women, husband and wife, mother and father; others may see slight differences; others great gaps between each. Some may also see little difference between woman, wife, mother or man, husband, father. It is important that each person be given a hearing.

Questions 1-5. Note that even though a couple may have no children, they can still answer these questions—and should do so. The reason is that essentially the questions help clarify what's important to you—so important you'd like to pass it on to others. And whether or not you have children, you still have a set of ideas about them that would be good to express before you have any (if ever).

Questions 6-12. Unless everyone has prepared these studies ahead of time you should simply suggest that all couples handle these questions at home, before the next study. You may want to open the second discussion by asking how these went.

These questions, of course, can only be asked if there are children of age to ask. Tell the group not to hesitate to ask even a two- or three-year-old. Even they can give interesting answers about what is going on inside their heads. Of course couples should feel free to modify the questions to suit the child being asked as long as the intent remains.

You may suggest to your group that they ask each child in the family separately so that they don't influence each other's answers. However, a family may feel it is better to discuss the questions as a group. This is perfectly acceptable since the purpose of the questions is not to take a Gallup poll but to get the family talking together over some important issues.

So you need not be limited by the questions listed.

Also mention that questions 10-11 can be used profitably even in one-child families.

There are a host of other topics that could and should be covered by a couple: use of money, vacations, spiritual development, relations with in-laws and so on. It is our hope that these few questions will stimulate further discussion within each family. Although *Handbook for Engaged Couples* by Bob and Alice Fryling (IVP) doesn't sound from its title like it might help, this valuable book can easily be adapted by married couples who want to continue their discussion of expectations in specific areas. You should find all but chapters 10-12 beneficial.

Study 2. Loving Yourself—Psalm 139
Purposes
☐ To see how God views and values us.
☐ To see how I view and value myself.
☐ To see what difference my own self-concept can make in my marriage.

If you want to, you can open this study by asking how the discussions went with children during the week. (See questions 6-12 in study one.)

Question 1. You may not need to ask question **1b** if the answers to **1a** already covered this. Also, be sure you do *not* read the passage until *after* you have discussed these questions.

Question 2. This is intended to give a quick overview of the whole psalm. The four parts of the psalm are then discussed in turn in the subsequent questions: God knows me (vv. 1-6); God is with me (vv. 7-12); God made me (vv. 13-18); God remakes me (vv. 19-24).

Questions 3-5. Another question you may find it appropriate to ask here (depending on the flow of discussion) is, "Are you afraid of knowing yourself? Why or why not?"

Question 4. See the note on the text for verse 5 if the group has trouble with this one.

Question 10. David knew he was far from perfect as the episode with Bathsheba clearly shows. This was no rhetorical request in verses 23-24. He did not want to share any of the God-defying ways of his enemies.

Study 3. One Family under God—Psalm 128
Purposes
☐ To discover the source of happiness for households.
☐ To consider how families can live happier lives.
Questions 1-2. These are addressed to husbands not because wives are not important or should not be asked these questions. Rather the psalm itself is addressed to husbands (note: "your wife," v. 3). However, there is no problem if discussion in your group also covers what makes wives happy. Your group might feel the same things make husbands and wives happy anyway. Nonetheless, there is more introspection these days among women than among men. So it might not hurt to balance this trend by focusing on men this time.
Question 3. Verse 1 is a case of parallelism—a poetic technique often used in Hebrew poetry in which the same thought is stated twice but in slightly different ways. Don't be upset, though, if some in your group think the two halves are different. Just be sure their reasons are good ones. You might ask, "If you don't do what God says, how can you say you respect and trust him?"
Question 4. This may (and should) be addressed to both men and women.
Questions 5-8. Question 5 asks the group to list work, wives and children. Questions 6-8 then discuss each of these in turn.

Study 4. One Plus One Equals One—Genesis 1:26-31; 2:15-25
Purposes
☐ To see the interdependency of husbands and wives.
☐ To discuss some basic elements of the marriage union.

This passage is covered again in study fifteen, so you may want to make notes after this study is over on how it went, who said what, what issues were left unresolved and the like. Then review these notes in preparation for study fifteen.

Question 1. Make sure you use follow-up questions that ask how dependence goes both ways: husbands depending on wives and wives depending on husbands. But don't seek exhaustive answers. Remember, this is just a thought starter.

Question 5. This is slightly different from question 1. Here the focus is on things a husband and wife do together rather than on what they do separately for each other.

Questions 6-9. Notice that these questions build on each other. It is important to discuss Adam's relationship with God, nature and Eve so the uniqueness of the last relationship can be seen clearly.

Study 5. Two to Submit—Ephesians 5:21-33
Purpose
□ To see that husband and wife submission are mutual though expressed differently.

Hang onto your hats, there's a good chance this will be your most controversial study. But don't be afraid of controversy itself or of strong differences of opinion. Try to present an atmosphere of openness and willingness to hear all sides. But don't be afraid to ask people to root their contentions in the passage. Your purpose is to see what Paul says here and not to bring in a myriad of outside resources and opinions. You may want to remind everyone before you start to stick to the passage!

Questions 4, 6, 9. We suggest that you make it clear to the group when a question is addressed to wives and when to husbands. Do not allow one spouse to speak for or evaluate the other. This is consistent with the fact that Paul addresses husbands and wives separately.

Question 8. In verse 33 Paul summarizes the different forms submission is to take for each spouse. Perhaps the reason for the difference is that while all human beings need both love and respect, women tend to feel more need for love, and men tend to feel more need for respect. Likewise, women can often express love easier than respect and vice versa. So Paul focuses on the tougher assignment for each.

Study 6. Being the Servant—Philippians 2:1-11
Purposes
☐ To consider Christ as servant.
☐ To understand more what it means to be a servant.
☐ To grow as servants in marriage.

Questions 3, 7. These are not easy questions to answer, given their personal nature. But they are important, nonetheless, to discuss openly. Your willingness to share honestly about your own marriage will encourage others to talk about the strengths and weaknesses in theirs.

Question 4. If a blackboard is available, you may want to jot down the answers people give for each of these three questions as they form a basis for comparison when question 7 comes up.

Question 8. If group members have not prepared ahead of time, have paper and pens available. Everyone should write silently for five minutes and then each couple should discuss their lists privately for another five minutes. At the end of this time, or when you get to this question if members have prepared ahead of time, have the group share about the value of this exercise.

Study 7. As Blood Is to the Body—Ephesians 4:1-3, 25-32
Purposes
☐ To consider what our communication should be like in order to lead a life worthy of our calling to Christ.
☐ To consider some ways of dealing with conflict in marriage.
☐ To see how communication can be improved in our marriage.

Question 1. If a blackboard is available, you may want to write Howe's statement on the board. Or refer people to page 29 of this guide.

If you wish, you may add, "How satisfied are you with the level of communication in your marriage?" Partners could write answers independently before discussing. In any case, this could be a threatening question. Consider beforehand if it is appropriate for your group.

Question 3. It is not necessary to, indeed you should probably discourage the group from, naming the names of these couples. The point is to characterize their marriages and thus suggest an example to learn from.

Questions 4-7. For group discussion you could precede these questions with "What other instructions does Paul give in verses 25-32?" and then list these on the board as they are mentioned by the group. You can then refer to them as you move through the details of the rest of the study. A group setting may not be the best place to discuss the second part of question 4; you should substitute, "In what ways is it difficult for you to speak the truth with your spouse?"

Question 8. Study nine will take up the issue of forgiveness in detail. A full discussion is not necessary here.

Question 9. If couples have prepared ahead of time, you could discuss the value of this exercise. If not, depending on the time you have, this can be done at the end of the study or later at home.

In the appendix are a number of other questions related to the ones in this study. At the end of the discussion you may want to direct interested couples to Table 2 on page 98. Although this is part of the guidelines for planning in marriage, these particular questions can be used independently.

Study 8. Drink Deeply, O Lovers—Song of Solomon 4:1—5:1

Purposes

☐ To see the importance of how Solomon and his bride

prepare for sex.
☐ To understand why we should not act as though sex were a right in marriage.
☐ To appreciate God's approval of sex in marriage.
☐ To identify ways one's sex life can be improved.

The entire Song of Solomon is worth reading and studying to gain a better appreciation of God's approval of sex in marriage. We have chosen one portion of the book to bring out a few principles related to the topic. This is by no means a comprehensive look, but we hope it will provide an opener for those who have not discussed it and some new insights for those who have.

This is one of the studies which may be particularly threatening or even embarrassing to some in your group. Be sensitive to this. We hope your group will have reached a level of openness and trust by this point that you can use the study basically as it stands. Nonetheless, you may wish to revise some questions or suggest that they be discussed by each couple afterward.

The Song of Soloman, or Song of Songs, has proved to be a difficult book to interpret. For centuries it was seen as an allegory for Christ and the church, perhaps quite appropriately given Paul's assessment in Ephesians 5. But, as recent scholars have stressed, the appropriateness of the allegory, if such it is, depends on the goodness of sex as God intended it. Another difficulty surrounding the book is the problem of determining the role and number of principal characters. One prominent view is that there are three: Solomon, the Shulammite and her shepherd-lover. The view assumed here is that there are only two principal characters—Solomon and the Shulammite. This position is supported by S. Craig Glickman among others (see For Further Reading at end of study).

For purposes of the study, it is probably best not to introduce the problem. If some members are familiar with an alternative view, acknowledge the possibilities and note that questions refer to the husband regardless of whether he is Solomon or the shepherd, and then move on. There is no need to debate this issue in the group.

Question 1. You may wish to use one of the following questions if you believe this approach question is too threatening.

Give one word to characterize your attitude toward sex in your marriage such as *duty, fun, fulfilling, squeamish, tolerated, great.* Explain if you wish.

On a scale of 1 to 10 (1 = poor; 10 = great) how would you rate your attitude toward sex in your marriage? Explain if you wish.

Question 9. Do not allow discussion to dwell on whether sex is or is not a right in marriage. In either case, the point is that the husband does not act like it is his right. He does not expect or demand it. Rather he acts as though he has to earn it, treating his wife with dignity in love. We should be treating our spouses the same—especially when it comes to sex.

Study 9. The Extent of Forgiveness—Matthew 18:21-35
Purposes
☐ To understand how Jesus' parable elaborates his teaching about forgiveness.
☐ To grow in understanding of how much we have been forgiven.
☐ To grow in forgiving our spouses.

This study and the next make a pair in more than one way. The next study continues right on in Matthew. So you may want to at least look at the next passage and the next study as you prepare for this one, especially if there are couples in your group who have divorced and are remarried. Since the next passage covers divorce, how much God has forgiven could be a very important prelude. Make sure the purposes of the study come through clearly, even if it means summarizing these points explicitly at the end. Likewise, this passage can offset any feelings of self-righteousness that the once-married may have.

Question 1. Several people may offer one-word replies. But seek fuller descriptions. You may ask, "Did you ever know a marriage like that? What was it like?" or, picking up on the discussion for study seven, "How might a lack of forgiveness affect communication?"

Question 3. Seek out answers that get to the root of human nature—selfishness, pride, self-righteousness and so on.

Question 12. You may want to have each person make an individual list and then take five minutes to discuss it with his or her spouse, unless they have already done this prior to the discussion.

Study 10. Until Divorce Do Us Part—Matthew 19:1-12
Purposes

☐ To allow couples to discuss their views on divorce before it actually becomes an issue for them.

☐ To consider Jesus' teaching on marriage and divorce.

☐ For each person to understand how he or she can better maintain a bond of marriage.

This may seem like a strange place to have a study on divorce—*before* various pressures on marriage are discussed. After all, isn't it the pressures that eventually cause divorce? But one of the main points of this study is that the issue of divorce can best be handled *before* these other pressures arise. If you have decided ahead of time that divorce is not an option and then a problem comes up, you have two choices: resolve the problem or live with it the rest of your lives. When divorce is not an option, the motivation to resolve the problem (rather than live with it) can be quite high. (See question 8.) Choosing never to divorce thus can help in handling other pressures.

There may be, however, as was mentioned above, some in your group who have not made such a decision, who in fact have been divorced. Note that this passage gives God's teaching on marriage for married couples—stay married! The passage covered in study nine gives God's teaching for those who did not obey that teaching—you are forgiven! Divorce is not the unforgivable sin; blasphemy against the Holy Spirit is. Don't let anyone in your group confuse the two.

Question 1. We strongly suggest you do ask these questions. You may, however, feel that **1a** is too threatening to ask in your group, especially right off the bat. If so, you might skip it and go right to **1b.** The two questions are really flip sides of the same record. But even if you skip **1a,** we encourage you to ask it at some appropriate point in the course of the study. This is often the heart of the problem for couples—they have never discussed divorce, when they would get one, when not. In today's world, divorce is an ever-present threat. Ignoring the threat does not make it any less potent. But in facing the threat, it can often be dealt with effectively.

Question 2. The first question helps identify the motives of the Pharisees in the interchange they are about to have with Jesus. The second helps identify our motives as we approach this passage. It could also help to squelch any who like the role of a devil's advocate by making them face themselves honestly.

Question 3-4. Rather than just touch on "two shall become one flesh" you may want to review or to ask a group member to review your discussion of study three on the three aspects of this verse: leaving father and mother, joining together, becoming one flesh. In any case, don't dwell long here but focus on **4a,** the pivotal point of the passage.

Your discussion in question **1** may mean that **4b** would be redundant. But if you skipped **1a** at the beginning, you may want to add it here, after **4b.**

Question 5. Don't skip **5c.** While those who live only by the law may be excused for divorcing, those who live by grace, whose hearts have been softened by the Spirit of God, are able to receive Christ's teaching.

Question 7. Christ is saying that if you choose to accept marriage, realize that you are also choosing to accept God's plan regarding divorce.

Study 11. Self-Serve—Luke 22:14-27
Purposes
☐ To understand the emphasis our society puts on self.
☐ To consider what Christ said about greatness and servant-hood.
☐ To evaluate myself as a servant in my marriage.
Questions 2-3. Be sensitive to the flow of discussion in your group. You may need to ask all these questions (plus some of your own) or you may need only a couple to help the group see how self-centered and defensive the disciples were in this time of crisis.

Study 12. The Harried Married—Psalm 23
Purposes
☐ To identify what the harried life is and why we are susceptible to it.
☐ To contrast the harried life with what the shepherd of Psalm 23 has to offer.
Psalm 23 is one of the most well-known, read, memorized and written-about passages in the Bible. It provides a striking contrast to the busyness most of our lives are filled with. Therefore you will want to allow a good amount of time for the approach questions, to set the stage so the contrast will stand out vividly. You may, in fact, want to add some questions to those already listed to get behind the initial responses. For example, "Why are we so uncomfortable when we aren't active?" Or, "Why aren't you able to say no when someone asks you to go somewhere or help with some project?"
Question 6. A shepherd might not only use his staff to fight off wild animals but to force his sheep to stay in the flock so they won't go astray.

Study 13. Rebellious Children—Luke 15:1-2, 11-32
Purposes
☐ To compare and contrast our parenting with God's parenting.

☐ To consider our relationship with God the Father.

Those in your group who have no chldren should certainly be made to feel free to participate—either out of how they respond to children now or in reflecting on how their parents have related to them as children.

Question 2. You may, for a change of pace, want to read this parable dramatically. You'll need someone to be the narrator, the father, the older son, the younger son and the servant. Don't neglect to read verses 1-2 which set the scene of the parable. (In verses 3-10 Jesus tells two shorter parables with similar points.) These verses also set the scene for questions 11-12 because Jesus was trying to say that the sinners were like the younger son and the Pharisees like the older.

Question 3. You may be able to skip **3b** if **3a** elicits a full response.

Question 7-8. Listing the specific acts the father makes in expressing his forgiveness of the son is important as a point of reference for how those in your group do or do not express it. For example, do you hug and kiss your child when you forgive? Do you restore full status as a son or daughter or continue to treat your child in a second-class way?

Question 11-12. These are important. Often parents have trouble parenting because they did not have good models to observe as they were being raised. And even now they have poor relations with their parents. They have not experienced a healthy parent-child relationship. But with God it is now possible to experience such a healthy relationship. Their relation with him can set the standard for how they relate to their own children rather than following their parents pattern.

Study 14. Money, Possessions, Security—Matthew 6:19-34
Purposes
☐ To consider what Christ has to say about money, posses·sions and security.
☐ To evaluate where my treasure is.

Question 1. Most people, if they are honest, will answer yes, they could live on half their present income. The point is to help people see that possessions aren't as critical as they might think. But then, that's the point of the whole discussion. Don't attempt to draw too many conclusions from this question. Just let it raise a few issues.

Question 3. To answer the first question here, you actually have to go to verse 33. Point the group there if they don't see it on their own.

Question 5. The point is, Does your heart follow your riches or do your riches follow your heart? Jesus says it's the former. Conclusion: Be careful where you put your riches, for your heart will surely place its concerns there.

Question 10. If your group moves easily into a discussion of worrying about the future before you get here—don't worry about it. Just skip these questions.

Study 15. Priorities in Marriage—Genesis 2:18—3:24; Mark 1:21-39

Purposes

☐ To consider God's priorities for us in marriage.

☐ To consider the consequences of having different priorities from God.

☐ To evaluate the place of prayer in how we determine our priorities.

If you took notes on how study four went in your group, be sure to review them as you prepare this study. They will give you clues as to what issues went unresolved and how people reacted to the passage in general. This discussion may give you a chance to round things out.

Question 3. As Trobisch says, since a marriage is full and complete without children, the implication is that the relationship between husband and wife takes precedence.

Question 7. Note that not only was Adam's and Eve's relationship with God disrupted but so was their relationship with themselves (v. 7), with each other (vv. 12, 16) and with nature (vv. 16-19).

Question 8. If most people unthinkingly respond that God has first priority in their lives, you may then want to ask them to sketch out quickly on a piece of paper how they normally spend the 168 hours in their week, such as 50 hours sleeping, 40 hours working, 14 hours eating, 10 hours recreating, etc. Ask a few to share their results. Then if appropriate, ask them, "How does this reflect God having first priority when only a few hours each week could be said to involve him directly?" If they can account for this, fine. At least they haven't answered question 8 unthinkingly. You may be able to think of some other way to get under the expected Christian response, a way that would fit your group better.

Question 11. The disciples evidently knew where to look to find Jesus, implying that he came to this "lonely place" often.

Be sure to mention that appendix A offers far more resources in setting priorities.

Study 16. Love Is—1 Corinthians 13

Purposes

□ To consider Paul's description of love.

□ To evaluate myself in my marriage in light of this description.

You may want to read 1 Corinthians 12—14 in preparation for this study to gain a better perspective on what Paul is saying. These chapters deal with the unity and diversity of the body of Christ especially in light of spiritual gifts. The last verse of chapter 12, then, helps set the contrast which Paul develops in 13:1-3 and 8-10.

Question 1. Obviously you could go all day on this one. Don't.

Question 4. If a blackboard is available, you might list in two columns what Paul says love is and what he says it is not.

Questions 5-6. These two phrases were chosen for discussion because they were less obvious than the others. Feel free to single out other phrases for special attention if a question arises in the group or in your own mind. Remember, you don't have to have all the answers anyway.

Question 10-11. Note that Paul does not emphasize how love feels to the person who loves but how it acts toward the person loved.

Appendix: Planning in Marriage

I can't jog alone. For a few days I'm fine—my enthusiasm is up, my commitment is high. I need to jog. I need a healthy, vigorous life. I will jog regularly each morning at 6 A.M. But after just a few days the bed begins to feel so very comfortable and the wind just a little too chilly to get up and don my tennies. So you see, I can't jog alone.

If I jog at all, it must be with someone else. I have to know that another person will be there, suffering with me because we think it's worthwhile to leave our pillows behind and greet the early morning by getting our aerobics points. I have to know I have made a commitment to another person who will also be there—or who will be there alone if I don't show. And if I can do it with a group—all the better.

The same will be true for many couples who want to plan. They won't be able to do it alone. Or if they do plan, they won't be able to follow through alone and actually execute the plan. After a few days or weeks, the old routine will start to feel all too comfortable. They need to have a group to which they can commit themselves, who will hold them responsible, who will motivate and encourage them. Your small group can be that group. You can use the plan outlined in Table 1 (p. 97) to help several married couples plan.

Table 5 (p. 128) gives a suggested schedule for a Friday-Saturday planning seminar that adapts the planning process described in Table 1 to a workshop context. We have two major goals for those who come to such a seminar: (1) during the seminar to complete a plan in one major category (financial, spiritual, social or the like) and (2) before the seminar is over, to set aside time on their calendars during which they

Table 5
Suggested Marriage Planning Seminar Schedule

Friday

7:15-7:30 P.M.	Gather and chat informally
7:30-8:00	Introduction and prayer
8:00-9:30	Garbage sessions as couples
9:30-10:00	Regather and talk over garbage session as a group

Saturday

8:45-9:00 A.M.	Gather and chat informally
9:00-9:15	Review as a group what the day will hold
9:15-10:30	Pray and complete Steps One and Two as couples (state overall purpose and describe the present)
10:30-11:00	Regather and talk over previous session as a group
11:00-Noon	Complete Step Three as couples (describe the ideal)
Noon-12:30 P.M.	Regather and talk over previous session as a group
12:30-1:30	Lunch
1:45-2:45	Complete Step Four (1)—brainstorm—as couples
2:45-3:00	Regather and talk over brainstorming as a group
3:00-3:20	Complete Step Four (2)—categorize alternatives—as couples
3:20-4:30	Complete Step Four (3-5)—evaluate alternatives, assign responsibilities, put them on a calendar—as couples for one category
4:30-5:00	Regather, talk over Step Four (2-5) as a group, pray, dismiss

will complete their plan in the other categories. There is not enough time to do all the planning in this twenty-four-hour period. But you can help people move through the process completely in one area so they could finish the others on their own.

During the introduction Friday night we let people know that these are our goals. We also review the material in the appendix, especially as it applies to the schedule of the seminar. Those who come should be encouraged to read the appendix ahead of time. They will work better knowing what to expect. Before the introduction ends and the garbage session begins, take time to pray for the seminar.

We close the introduction by explaining briefly the purpose and nature of the garbage session. Couples then discuss the questions found on page 98. You will need a facility that allows couples to be totally private. Separate rooms with doors that can be closed are a must so that couples will be free to discuss their most private thoughts. (The rooms are also needed for the sessions on Saturday.) We do, however, warn couples that we plan to drop in on each of them once during the hour (and during the other hours they work alone on Saturday) to see how they are doing and to ask if they have hit a roadblock with which we could help or if they have any questions or problems. If there are no problems or questions, we move on. If there are problems, we do what we can to help discussion keep going.

Regathering to talk things over after each of these one-to-one sessions is very important. Many couples will have found the session difficult and may think they were the only ones who had a tense time. It can be very reassuring to find out they were not alone and to hear how other couples also work through conflicts. We've used some of the following questions to start the discussion:

How did it go?

Was it hard to get started? Why or why not?

What else did you find difficult?

Did you learn anything about yourselves? If so, what?

Did anything exciting happen? Tell us about it.

We use these same questions during each of the regathering sessions during the seminar with minor alterations to suit the session just completed. At the close of each regathering we then review what is coming up next.

Besides reading the appendix, another assignment you might give for each couple to complete before attending is to write out answers to the questions on pages 99-100 regarding what their marriage is actually like now. This will save a lot of time in the first session Saturday morning, allowing the other aspects of steps one and two to be discussed more fully.

A word of warning. You will find it very difficult to lead

any others through the planning process described in the appendix unless you have first done it yourself. You, unfortunately, will not have the help of others working with you unless you pair up with one other couple and try it with just four of you. We hope you will find it worthwhile.